AMERICAN AUTHORS AND CRITICS SERIES

GENERAL EDITOR

JOHN MAHONEY

University of Detroit

HENRY JAMES   Portrait by John Singer Sargent, 1913.

HENRY

JAMES

An Introduction and Interpretation

LYALL H. POWERS

University of Michigan

HOLT, RINEHART AND WINSTON, INC.

New York · Chicago · San Francisco · Atlanta · Dallas

Montreal · Toronto · London · Sydney

Permission has been granted by the National Portrait Gallery (London) to reproduce the portrait of Henry James by John Singer Sargent.

Permission has been granted by Charles Scribner's Sons to quote excerpts from *Henry James: Autobiography*, ed. F. W. Dupee, 1956; *The Letters of Henry James*, ed. Percy Lubbock, 1920; and *The Art of the Novel: Critical Prefaces by Henry James*, ed. R. P. Blackmur, 1934.

Permission has been granted by Oxford University Press (New York) to quote excerpts from *The Notebooks of Henry James*, ed. F. O. Matthiessen and Kenneth B. Murdock, 1947. Paperback edition published by George Braziller in 1953.

ABOUT THE AUTHOR

LYALL H. POWERS, professor of English at the University of Michigan, has published essays on Henry James and other English and American writers in the major scholarly journals. He revised the *Viking Portable Henry James;* edited *Henry James's Major Novels: Essays in Criticism;* wrote a monograph on James's life and works; edited a collection of essays and reviews of *The Portrait of a Lady;* and compiled a bibliography of works by and about James. He is presently working on a study of the works of William Faulkner.

For Christopher, Graham, and Victoria

PREFACE

THIS BOOK attempts simply to fulfill the promise of its title: to extend to the reader an introduction to Henry James's life and career, and to offer an interpretation of his work. It is no longer necessary (as it once was) to plead the case of Henry James, for he is now clearly recognized as one of the foremost practitioners of the art of fiction in English. Scholars have made much progress in determining the sources upon which he drew and the philosophical ideas that inform his work; critics have done much to explicate the complexities of his stories and to evaluate his artistry; and fellow authors have acclaimed his achievement.

James enjoyed a long career and the range of his endeavor was broad. In this study, therefore, I have had to leave largely untouched his contribution to travel literature, to the belletristic essay, and the literary review. I have chosen to concentrate on his prose fiction—where we find him at his very best—and on the most immediately relevant of his other writing, chiefly literary criticism. The information and critical opinion offered here will be of interest and assistance to the reader of any portion of James's work and will enable him better to understand what James is "all about" both generally and in specific instances. I have attempted, in the biographical chapter and the subsequent chapters on the literature itself, to demonstrate the fundamental unity of James's moral attitude and the consistency of aim in his artistic endeavor; at the same time, I have tried to accommodate the variety of his production and evaluate the constant development within his long career. The two, as will be seen, are not incompatible. Thus, although not every one of James's numerous stories is specifically discussed here, the book nevertheless provides a reliable context of assistance for the reader interested in any particular work. All of the major novels are discussed, of course, and many of the principal novellas and short stories.

I am grateful for financial assistance in the preparation of the manuscript given by the Horace H. Rackham Foundation of the University of Michigan. And I owe a special debt of gratitude to my wife for her encouragement and understanding.

L. H. P.

Ann Arbor, Michigan
September 1969

CONTENTS

Preface   vii
Chronology   x
Introduction   1
1. Life and Career   9
   "Those Untried Years"   9
   The Experimental Middle Years   17
   The Major Phase   27
2. Fiction I: The International Theme   40
   The Portrait of a Lady   60
   Other Stories of the Middle Years   75
   The Major Phase   79
3. Fiction II: The Dilemma of the Artist   100
4. Fiction III: Related Themes   117
5. James's Esthetics   126
6. A Note on Narrative Technique   137
   Conclusion   148

   Selected Bibliography   150
   Index   161

CHRONOLOGY

1843 Henry James born, April 15, at 2 Washington Place, New York City, a second son.

1843–1844 First trip to Europe.

1845–1855 Family lives in New York City and Albany, New York.

1855–1858 Family lives in various places in Europe. Henry, a "devourer of libraries," begins youthful writings.

1858 Family returns to America, lives at Newport, Rhode Island.

1859 Family makes return visit to Europe.

1860–1861 Family returns to live at Newport. Henry studies art with William Morris Hunt; receives "obscure hurt."

1862–1863 Henry enrolled at Harvard Law School.

1864 Family moves to Boston. Henry publishes first critical essay and first short story.

1866 Family establishes home in Cambridge, Massachusetts.

1869–1870 Henry makes first trip alone to Europe. Hears of death of his first and enduring love, his cousin Minny Temple.

1871 First novel, *Watch and Ward,* published serially in *Atlantic Monthly.*

1872–1874 Henry travels to Europe with sister Alice.

1874 Returns to New York for the winter.

1875 Publishes first book of fiction, *A Passionate Pilgrim and Other Tales,* and first travel book, *Transatlantic Sketches.* First attempt at expatriation: moves to Paris, where he meets the "grandsons of Balzac."

1876 First novel published in book form, *Roderick Hudson.* Moves to London.

1877 *The American.* Revisits Paris; winters in Rome.

1878 *Watch and Ward* in book form. First book of criticism, *French Poets and Novelists.*

1879 First "best seller," *Daisy Miller;* first critical biography, *Hawthorne.* Has full social calendar in London.

1881 *The Portrait of a Lady,* his first masterpiece. Returns to the United States.

1882 Death of his mother, February; death of his father, December.

1883   Returns to England to begin definite expatriation. First collection of his fiction, 14 vols.

1886   *The Bostonians* and *The Princess Casamassima*. Takes a flat in London, De Vere Mansions (later De Vere Gardens).

1888   *Partial Portraits.*

1890   *The Tragic Muse*. Begins experiment of writing for the stage.

1891   Dramatized version of *The American* produced.

1894–1895   Contributes three stories to *The Yellow Book.*

1895   Play *Guy Domville* produced in London; first-night catastrophe determines James to end his theatrical experiment.

1896   Spends summer near Rye, Sussex, and discovers Lamb House.

1897   *The Spoils of Poynton; What Maisie Knew.*

1898   *The Turn of the Screw; In the Cage*. James begins living in Lamb House.

1899   *The Awkward Age.*

1901   *The Sacred Fount.*

1902   *The Wings of the Dove.*

1903   *The Ambassadors;* group biography, *William Wetmore Story and His Friends.*

1904   *The Golden Bowl*. Returns to the United States after 21-year absence, to arrange publication of collected edition of his fiction.

1905   Lecture tour of the United States and Canada.

1906   Returned to Lamb House, works at preparation of his novels and tales for the collected edition.

1907   *The Novels and Tales of Henry James,* the "New York Edition," published by Charles Scribner's Sons; *The American Scene.*

1908   Contributes chapter to composite novel, *The Whole Family;* play, *The High Bid,* produced in Edinburgh and London.

1909   Suffers protracted nervous illness.

1910   Visits Bad Nauheim with brother William. Returns to the United States with William, who dies in August.

1911   Receives honorary degree from Harvard University; returns to Lamb House.

1912   Takes flat in London at 21 Carlyle Mansions, Cheyne Walk; receives honorary degree from Oxford University.

1913   *A Small Boy and Others,* first autobiographical volume.

1914   *Notes of a Son and Brother,* second autobiographical volume; *Notes on Novelists and Some Other Notes;* begins civilian war work and writing.

1915 Naturalized a British subject.

1916 Awarded Order of Merit; dies, February 28; funeral service in Chelsea Old Church; ashes interred in Cambridge, Massachusetts.

1917 Two unfinished novels published, *The Ivory Tower* and *The Sense of the Past;* and unfinished autobiographical volume, *The Middle Years.*

INTRODUCTION

Henry James was one of the most prolific as well as one of the greatest writers America has produced. He wrote some two dozen novels, a like number of novellas, scores of short stories, a dozen plays, several books of criticism both practical and theoretical, several books of travel literature, a thick and rich notebook, and literally thousands of letters. His most important achievement, however, was in the realm of prose fiction—both as practitioner and as critic; and while the scope of this volume does not permit an attempt to do full justice to James's total accomplishment, some justice can be done to his achievement in the art of fiction. He generally is considered to have contributed generously to the development of modern prose fiction both by precept and by example—by theoretic criticism in such pieces as "The Art of Fiction" (1884), "The Future of the Novel" (1914), and the eighteen prefaces he wrote for the collected edition of his novels and tales in 1907–1909, and by the brilliant example of the novels and tales themselves.

James is perhaps best known as the author of stories dealing with the "international scene," the transatlantic intercourse of American and European society and culture. It is true that he used that phenomenon as it appeared during the second half of the nineteenth and the beginning of the twentieth centuries; indeed, he was the first writer of any stature to make the international scene a major matter in fiction, and he left an interesting and detailed account of the experiences, the characters, and the settings that figured prominently in that scene. Consequently, he has sometimes been regarded (and sometimes dismissed) as principally a novelist of manners—as a writer whose value lies in an accurate rendering of life as it was, as a creator of slightly fictionalized historical vignettes—a kind of transoceanic local-colorist. The first point to be grasped, therefore, is that James's virtue as a novelist lies *ultimately* in his ability to express, *through the medium of* the international scene, profound and enduring truths

1

about the career of mankind. His international stories, like all of his fiction, are basically concerned with Man in the world, and only incidentally and superficially with the American in Europe three-quarters of a century ago. Satisfying as the surface story of a given Jamesian novel or tale may be, its value lies, at last, in the ideas about humanity expressed by that surface; the story—however rich, complex, and engrossing—is in a sense a metaphor that expresses the Jamesian truth. This is not to say that he wrote allegory: he objected to the allegorical quality in the work of his famous predecessor Nathaniel Hawthorne, asserting that allegory spoiled a good story. The point is, simply, that James recorded with verifiable fidelity the international (and other) scenes as he knew them *not for their own sake* but for the ulterior purpose of expressing truths about us all.

The source of those truths is to be found primarily in the household in which he was raised, of course, and in the spirit of the age as it was during his formative years. James belongs in the liberal Protestant tradition, shared by such writers as John Milton and William Blake, by Emerson and Hawthorne, and in which his own father, Henry James, Senior—probably the strongest single influence on him—was securely founded. It is a tradition that firmly stresses the importance of individual freedom and personal responsibility, that is acutely sensitive to the dangers of authoritarian control, that cherishes spiritual values and scorns the transient and deceptive delights of the *merely* worldly. Not an ascetic tradition, it therefore does not encourage a turning away from the world: indeed, it expressly requires that the world be heartily and bravely accepted— for what it is. "I cannot praise a fugitive and cloister'd virtue, unexercis'd and unbreath'd, that never sallies out and sees her adversary," wrote Milton in his *Areopagitica*. "Assuredly we bring not innocence into the world, we bring impurity much rather: that which purifies us is triall, and triall is by what is contrary. That vertue therefore which is but a youngling in the contemplation of evill, and knows not the utmost that vice promises to her followers, and rejects it, is but a blank vertue, not a pure; her whitenesse is but an excrementall whitenesse."

That sentiment is very close to the burden of William Blake's *Songs of Innocence and Experience*. And Hawthorne's *The Marble Faun*, for example, explicitly tests Milton's moral attitude: Hilda's "purity" is very nearly the "excrementall whitenesse" mentioned in the *Areopagitica,* and the "triall" of Miriam and Donatello has quite the effect of purifying them in Milton's sense—and Miriam has helped Donatello through that development from initial innocence, through experience to a higher innocence, which Blake indicates, in his *Songs* and elsewhere, as the necessary career of man. Similarly, Emerson constantly emphasized the importance and necessity of experience, of confronting life resolutely and of bravely relying on oneself alone. For Emerson, to rely on oneself (properly understood) was to rely on the spark of divinity within.

James gives no explicit expression of belief in the divinity of man (although he came reasonably close to doing so late in his life in "Is There a Life After Death?" published in 1910), yet that is constantly the implication of the ethical attitude expressed in his fiction. He shared Emerson's view of the importance of self-reliance and of the Socratic prerequisite of self-knowledge: to know the needs and desires of one's true self and to rely upon the urges that follow therefrom should be each person's chief concern and guide. James cherished the value of individual human integrity and saw the development of each individual's potential as the greatest good. Consequently, whatever contributed to that development he considered good, and whatever impeded it evil.

In James's view, those impediments to human development were most obviously the various laws of man's creation that dictated systems of behavior: the traditions of social history, the conventions of civilized society, the rituals of institutionalized religion, and the regulations of ethical codes. The figure of authority, the voice of duty—these made up the Jamesian *bête-noire,* which bears a close resemblance to Blake's evil figure of the Father-Priest-King. The villains in James's fiction, therefore, are the instruments by which these hindrances are enacted—anyone who willfully interferes with the realization of another's human potential. Like Hawthorne, James considered the intrusive manipulator of human lives to be the most hateful and diabolical of creatures. Sometimes villainous behavior of this sort is the result of a mistaken benevolence—a busybody desire to be helpful. (That is the case with one of James's best-known characters, the wretched governess in *The Turn of the Screw.*) And often James's protagonists are the victims of their own villainy: they will not listen to the voice of their own (apparently divine) soul, but attempt to follow the dictates of authority, of duty externally imposed. On occasion, this suicidal self-deception takes the

form of an inflated evaluation of innocence, which amounts to a refusal to accept the responsibility of adulthood; it is a cherishing
of what Milton called "blank vertue."

Real virtue, then, consists in the quest of full experience, in the
facing of life secure in self-knowledge and self-trust, and with eyes
wide open—especially to see all that life can offer of both good and
evil. Of course James's assumption is that we live in a fallen world
once good but now shot through with evil. The good man must learn
to recognize evil—to recognize it in and of itself, not according to
the prejudgment encouraged by whatever system of laws. And he
must not turn aside from evil—which is the case of the heroine of
Blake's *Thel*—but confront and overcome it by seeing the worst that
it can do and yet not flinching. Moral success awaits him who lives
through the world's evils by refusing to succumb to them, by eschew-
ing the merely material rewards of the transient and perishable world
and committing himself to the enduring spiritual values.

Since he shared the idea (as old as St. Paul) that one does not
achieve goodness by regulating behavior according to laws and systems, James is much more concerned with how to *be* good than how
to *do* good. What one *is* matters most; the hypocrite may do good
without being good, and is finally unreliable. In this James shares the
attitude of Matthew Arnold, expressed most graphically in his contrast of Hellenism and Hebraism, that the enlightened consciousness
which contemplates life as it is infinitely surpasses in goodness the
active conscience that worries one into the attempt to avoid evil
and even sometimes into doing good. Behind this belief lay again
Blake's scorn of slave-morality—refraining from certain acts through
fear of punishment rather than embracing what one *wants* because
he truly sees its good. But James had had this idea impressed upon
him from his earliest years by the gentle advice his father gave him
and his brother William. He recalls that "What was marked in our
father's prime uneasiness in presence of any particular form of success we might . . . propose to invoke was that it bravely, or with
such inward assurance, dispensed with any suggestion of an alternative. What we were to do instead was just to *be* something, something
unconnected with specific doing, something free and uncommitted,
something finer in short than being *that*, whatever it was, might consist of." [1]

James's moral concern was directed to the individual human

[1] "Notes of a Son and Brother" (1914), *Henry James, Autobiography*, ed.
F. W. Dupee (New York: Criterion Books, 1956), p. 268.

consciousness. He was interested in spiritual or psychological moral health, believing that good action will follow from him who *is* good. He felt that successful human intercourse would result in a society comprised of individuals who knew and trusted themselves and could therefore respect the human integrity of others—individuals who could, then, truly love their neighbors as themselves. Of course James was not simply a naïve idealist. He knew well that traditions, conventions, and manners were necessary for the smooth functioning of civilized society—that one was obliged to *do* things in certain acceptable ways in order that civilized human intercourse be possible. But he wanted to sound the warning reminder that to give oneself up to any institution was to lose something of one's independence; to give oneself up too easily or too completely was to risk losing all, to run the danger of becoming a kind of "hollow man" who is nothing but his manners. James saw clearly that compromise is necessary. The ultimate value is always the individual, but he must adapt conventional manners to himself in such a way as to have them express *himself* truly. To refuse the necessary compromise is as destructive as to yield completely—as the case of Daisy Miller most dramatically demonstrates. In a very real sense, all of James's fiction is devoted to an examination of the terms on which the compromise is possible. One of our greatest heroes in American literature is Huckleberry Finn, whom we admire precisely because he is so uncompromising, because he will not come to terms with society; but poor Huck leaves finally to travel into the West, seeking his uncompromised freedom, and is committed even more desperately than Conrad's Lord Jim to a perpetual westward retreat. James was more realistic: he knew that the woods of the territory were "lovely, dark, and deep," but that in this life adult man has his promises to keep and many miles to go.

In many ways, then, James's fiction can speak directly to us and to our time. He is in sympathy with those who chafe at the bonds of authority and balk at the stern commands of duty and conscience; and he shares fully our profound respect for the rights of the individual. He is unmistakably an "apostle of freedom," yet his fiction encourages recognition of the responsibility that real freedom demands and of the necessity of accepting commitment to life. He makes the futility and destructiveness of the "drop-out" philosophy abundantly clear. As a dying lover, in one of James's novels, says to his desperate beloved who does not want to continue living without him: "In life there's love." It is a simple but profoundly true expression.

James is likewise an apostle of love, for love and freedom go hand in hand; many of his stories, consequently, are love stories.

It is sometimes thought, nevertheless, that on one or two of these counts James singularly fails. How can it be said that James is opposed to the "drop-out" philosophy when hero after Jamesian hero is an arresting example of the art of renunciation? Christopher Newman (*The American*) has the means of avenging himself against the Bellegardes for refusing him their daughter, and declines to use it; Isabel Archer (*The Portrait of a Lady*) escapes the domination of her villainous husband and then has several opportunities for "freedom," but refuses them all and returns to that husband; Lambert Strether (*The Ambassadors*) has his pick, apparently, of the attractive women at the end of his novel, but refuses them all to return to America alone; Merton Densher (*The Wings of the Dove*) can enjoy an enormous inheritance or the delights of marriage to lusty Kate Croy—and just possibly both—yet turns down both; and so on through a long list. But in every case, it is merely material advantage that is renounced; and indeed the case is always so presented as finally to suggest that acceptance of the reward would in itself be a kind of "drop-out." It is James's way of cautioning against putting faith in the perishable, in those goods that fade and ultimately fail to satisfy. In many such cases, obviously, the reward is an attractive mate. And here arises another objection.

How can it be claimed (demands the modern reader of current fare from *The Tropic of Cancer* to *The American Dream*) that James writes love stories when a kiss is as rare as a karate blow in his fiction? Admittedly James is reticent about the fact of sex—and doubtless there was a strong "Puritan" streak in him—but at least he is able to distinguish between the merely physical involvement and true love that depends on a metaphysical (or spiritual) component. He invites us to consider the threat of sexual *possession* as we would that of any other form of possession in human intercourse. (James is fundamentally very close to D. H. Lawrence in this respect.) To be thus enslaved, James implies, is little different from being enslaved by a similar commitment to *things*—a major theme of *The Spoils of Poynton*. For all his reticence about the fact of sex, James generously considers its effects again and again in his fiction: what it *means* is more important, psychologically, than what it simply is. What it means is, of course, a much more complex matter, and infinitely more difficult to express faithfully, than the simple fact itself.

With this arises perhaps the most common objection to James: he is verbose and oblique and indirect. He just will not up and tell you, as say Ernest Hemingway ups and tells. James thought long and wrote much about how fiction ought to be written—if it was to succeed as an interesting representation of life. He felt that a well-written story ought to strike you as experiences in real life do—that is, directly and without explanatory comment and, particularly, with as much of life's complexity and richness as possible. Consequently, the novel must *show* rather than tell and interpret, and it must show all the complicated and various attendant circumstances (or seem to show them all)—especially when what it had to show was not only things (people and places and handsome scenes) but typical human reactions and motivations. James was really ahead of his time in his interest in psychology—in *why* people did as they did, rather than simply in *what* they did. In complaining against readers who demanded "adventure"—that is, flashing swords and crackling pistols, rapes and rumpus—James quietly made a plea for the "psychological adventure" as a sound subject for fiction:

> And what *is* adventure, when it comes to that . . . ? It is an adventure—an immense one—for me to write this little article; and for a Bostonian nymph to reject an English duke is an adventure only less stirring, I should say, than for an English duke to be rejected by a Bostonian nymph. . . . A psychological reason is, to my imagination, an object adorably pictorial; to catch the trick of its complexion—I feel as if that idea might inspire one to Titianesque efforts. There are few things more exciting to me, in short, than a psychological reason, and yet, I protest, the novel seems to me the most magnificent form of art.[2]

Obviously James is addressing himself to both points: (1) that a novel ought to *show*, as if dramatically or pictorially, its subject; and (2) that the psychological element is as important a concern for the writer as any other. But the problem for the psychological realist is precisely to "catch the trick of its complexion" by means of words alone. To do more than suggest the highlights—that is, "he was angry," "she was hungry," "they were dishonestly flattering"—requires a certain number of words carefully chosen and cunningly arranged. Hence the obliquity and indirectness of James's style, which is so often mistaken for verbosity. Such a style does

---

[2] "The Art of Fiction," *The Future of the Novel,* ed. Leon Edel (New York: Vintage Books, 1956), p. 23.

not make for "easy" reading—just rewarding reading. Subtlety and
complexity prove to be more satisfying—in good fiction as in good
jokes; and, as in so many worthwhile endeavors, the rewards offered
the reader of James's fiction are commensurate with the effort he
is willing to expend. A James story does not promise a cheap and
easy pleasure; the best things in life never do.

LIFE AND CAREER

"THOSE UNTRIED YEARS"

ORTUNATE IN HIS BIRTH, Henry James could hardly have improved on his original situation if he had arranged it himself,
for it was in many ways a most auspicious beginning for the future
man of letters. He was born, April 15, 1843, just off Washington
Square in New York City, into the third American generation of a
family already well-to-do. His grandfather, an Irish immigrant, was
one of the wealthiest men in America when he died, and he left his
children independently wealthy. Thus, Henry James's father—also
named Henry—was free to devote himself to theological and philosophical studies and to the education and cultural improvement of
his children. The children knew little of what was "normal" school-
ing among their young compatriots: not only did their father move
them from school to school in America, he transported them abroad
early and often. The elder Henry James was partial to European
education—education in the broadest sense—as he explained to his
friend Ralph Waldo Emerson in a letter of 1849:

. . . looking upon our four stout boys, who have no play room within
doors, and import shocking bad manners from the street, with much
pity, we gravely ponder whether it would not be better to go abroad for
a few years with them, allowing them to absorb French and German
and get a better sensuous education than they are likely to get here.[1]

Henry James's education was characterized by a strong cosmo-
politan note, as he was put to school in various institutions in England, Switzerland, and France. At the Collège Impériale in Boulogne
he had as a schoolmate the young Benoît Constant Coquelin who
was to become one of the outstanding actors of the French theater
during the latter half of the century. By the time Henry was seven-

[1] Quoted in Leon Edel, *Henry James: The Untried Years, 1843–1870* (Philadelphia and New York: J. B. Lippincott Company, 1953), p. 118.

teen he had spent almost a third of his young life abroad; his "sensuous education" had been properly founded; he had fully absorbed the "European virus."

The James home in America, furthermore, breathed an atmosphere of culture, of ideas in ferment, of the world of books and art. Henry James, Senior, enjoyed something of a reputation as a Swedenborgian religious philosopher; and among his friends and close aquaintances were numbered many of the leading figures of the day, both American and European—Emerson, Carlyle, Hawthorne, Thackeray, Thoreau, Bronson Alcott, and many others. The children, especially Henry and his elder brother, William, were encouraged to join in the discussions, to sharpen their young wits and discover their own nascent ideas. And always, of course, there was the gently dominant influence of their father. Henry would recall, years later, the effect on him of his father's "remarkable genius"; in the autobiographical *Notes of a Son and Brother* he pays this tribute to "Father's Ideas" (significant capitals!).

> . . . what comes back to me, to the production of a tenderness and an admiration scarce to be expressed, is the fact that though we thus easily and naturally lived with them and indeed, as to their more general effects, the colour and savour they gave to his talk, breathed them in and enjoyed both their quickening and their embarrassing presence, to say nothing of their almost never less than amusing, we were left as free and unattacked by them as if they had been so many droppings of gold and silver coin on tables and chimney-pieces, to be "taken" or not according to our sense and delicacy, that is our felt need and felt honour.[2]

The James family established their home in Newport, Rhode Island, in 1860, and thus the transatlantic shuttle ceased. They had spent 1858–1859 in Newport and would live there during the early years of the Civil War. The Newport phase of Henry's young life was brief but important. Newport itself exerted a strong appeal: it seemed an ideal combination of the values of Europe and of America—the good of both without the ills of either. "The old town seemed indeed," writes Leon Edel, James's brilliant biographer, "with its crooked streets and small buildings, its old wharves, its association with Bishop Berkeley, its historic cemeteries, to be a bit of Europe or an European outpost in the soil of America." It was

---

[2] *Autobiography,* pp. 330–331.

furthermore "a corner of the eighteenth century that had lingered into the nineteenth."[3] But Newport was further endeared to Henry because of the people he knew there. To begin with there were the Temple cousins, four orphaned girls of whom Mary (Minny) was the favorite. Minny Temple was a most popular young lady among members of Henry's circle, and the great love of his life. There was also Thomas Sergeant Perry, already a young bibliophile, later a critic and editor, who became Henry's first intimate friend; and, John La Farge, a painter who was later to do illustrations for James's famous novella *The Turn of the Screw*. La Farge's important influence, in addition to enlivening Henry's sense for the visual arts, was to initiate him into the world of French literature: he lent him copies of the *Revue des deux mondes* and, in 1860, introduced him to the work of Honoré de Balzac. James's admiration for the great French novelist was immediately awakened and persisted throughout his life. He came to recognize Balzac as his "greatest master" and confessed, in his sixties, that he had learned more of the mystery of the craft of fiction from him than from anyone else.

Into the calm of the James's Newport life erupted the shock of the Civil War; the firing on Fort Sumter coincided almost exactly with Henry's eighteenth birthday. The two younger James brothers, Bob and Wilky, fought in the ranks of the Union army, and Wilky was gravely wounded. Henry was unable to enlist, for in the autumn of 1861 a minor injury incurred while serving as a volunteer fireman laid him up: it was a mild but annoying injury—a slipped disc, a sacroiliac or muscular strain—that not only rendered him unfit for military service but returned to plague him periodically all the rest of his life. With the physical annoyance there was also a nagging sense of guilt over his failure of military service that also persisted, and that accounts in part for his energetic and generous participation as a civilian during World War I—a kind of compensation.

He followed William to Harvard in 1862, ostensibly to study law; but he spent his time mainly in pursuing whatever other studies appealed to him and, most important, in writing. For the die was already cast: he must write, and would follow no other vocation. He attained his majority in 1864, and as if to celebrate that important milestone he made his literary debut—the first publication of what would be a long and prolific career. It is further significant that his literary debut was marked by a dual publication—first a

[3] *Untried Years*, p. 139.

short story, "A Tragedy of Error," and then a critical essay,
["Nassau W. Senior's] Essays in Fiction." For Henry James was
to affect the world of letters both as author and as critic. Henceforth the story of his life is largely the story of his career as a
writer: in a very real sense the whole of his life was devoted to the
art of fiction. One of his early fictional characters may almost be
said to speak for him when he says, "Just as the truly religious soul
is always at worship, the genuine artist is always in labor."

It was also singularly appropriate that James's literary career
should begin in the same year that Nathaniel Hawthorne's came to
an end. As Balzac was the principal foreign literary influence on
James, Hawthorne was the principal American. The conjunction of
the end of Hawthorne's career and the beginning of James's is
somehow symbolic—it was as though the mantle of the master passed
directly to his young successor, the line of succession unbroken.

In the next five years James published over a dozen short stories
—"The Story of a Year" in 1865 was the first he signed, Henry
James, Jr.—more than twenty reviews (all but one unsigned), and
his first play, *Pyramus and Thisbe.* His writing led him to the
acquaintance and friendship of James Russell Lowell and Charles
Eliot Norton of *The North American Review,* William Dean Howells
and James T. Field of the *Atlantic,* and E. L. Godkin of *The Nation.*
His introduction to prominent figures of the literary world was extended during his fourteen-month trip to Europe in 1869–1870. He
dined with Ruskin, lunched with Dickens, spent an evening with
William Morris, and a Sunday afternoon with George Eliot. But his
introduction to Rome seems to have surpassed all: "Here I am then
in the Eternal City," he wrote to William. "At last—for the first
time—I live!" He confessed that he had gone "reeling and moaning
thro' the streets, in a fever of enjoyment." [4] The visits to George
Eliot and to Italy were undertaken in part to satisfy Minny Temple;
it was all in a sense "Minny's voyage," and Henry was her vicar,
but the plan was for her to come over from America and join him
in Italy. The plan was never carried out: in March of 1870 James
received word that Minny had died. His letters in response to that
news show that he was deeply shocked by his loss. Almost half a
century later he recorded, in *Notes of a Son and Brother,* the sense

[4] *The Letters of Henry James,* ed. Percy Lubbock, 2 vols. (New York: Charles
Scribner's Sons, 1920), I, 24.

of that death: "her death made a mark that must stand here for a . . . conclusion. We felt it together [William and I] as the end of our youth." [5]

But this sad year of conclusion was also a year of beginning for Henry as a writer of travel literature: *The Nation* published four pieces from his pen in 1870, including one on Newport. In the next couple of years he also published important articles on Hawthorne, George Eliot, and Ivan Turgenev, and his first short story dealing with the problems of being an artist, "The Madonna of the Future." During another visit of a few months in Rome he met Fanny Kemble, daughter of the famous Shakespearean actor Charles Kemble. She was to be James's frequent companion at the theater, and she was a most fruitful raconteur: his Notebooks indicate that Fanny Kemble provided him with more "germs" for stories than anyone else during their friendship of more than twenty years. In Rome he was also introduced to the American artist colony by his compatriot the sculptor William Wetmore Story. It was at Story's too that he met Matthew Arnold, a favorite of James's since his teens—in 1865 he had published a review of Arnold's *Essays in Criticism*. Arnold's influence on James was more considerable than has yet been generally recognized, and is already quite discernible in James's first "international" novel, *Roderick Hudson* (1875). Indeed, the whole Roman experience made a strong impression on the young American writer: here in Rome he found the setting and the very characters of Hawthorne's last novel, *The Marble Faun*. Appropriately he set to work the next spring on his own novel of American artists in Rome. *Roderick Hudson* was actually his second novel—*Watch and Ward* had been published serially in the *Atlantic* in 1871—but James would always consider it as "really" his first, and it occupies the first volume of the definitive edition of his works. Percy Lubbock aptly remarks of *Roderick Hudson* that "its composition marks the definite end of Henry James's literary apprenticeship." [6] James had entered his thirties.

The year of *Roderick Hudson*, 1875, was a year of decision for Henry James, a turning point in his career. During that year he published two more "firsts"—*A Passionate Pilgrim and Other Tales*, his first volume of short stories, and *Transatlantic Sketches*, his first volume of travel literature—and a significant essay on Balzac. At this time he was apparently wrestling with the problem of whether

[5] *Autobiography*, p. 544.
[6] *Letters*, I, 14.

to remain in his native land like his master Hawthorne and his friend
Howells or to take up residence in Europe where, as he had written
William, he had first begun to "live." His reading of Balzac, the
charm of George Eliot, his father's admiration of Turgenev (which
he shared), his newly awakened interest in Flaubert and the other
"grandsons of Balzac" (as he considered them), and the effect of that
"sensuous education" he had received abroad from his tenderest
years—all these factors combined to determine James to make the
choice of expatriation to Europe. In the fall of the year he moved
to the Latin Quarter of Paris; and except for the winter and spring
of 1881–1882 and several months of 1883, he would spend the next
three decades of his life in Europe.

He remained in Paris a scant year. An exchange of letters with
Ivan Turgenev, himself an expatriate in Paris, gained James an
introduction to the Flaubert circle of writers—Zola, Daudet, the
remaining Goncourt, young Maupassant, Turgenev, and others.
It was a momentous occasion for James, although the fruits of the
association would not become apparent until almost a decade later.
In the meantime he removed to London, just off Piccadilly, where
his social circle widened immeasurably. His letters home bristle with
famous names: "Yesterday [that is, March 28, 1877] I dined with
Lord Houghton—with Gladstone, Tennyson, Dr. Schliemann (the
excavator of old Mycenae, etc.) and half a dozen other men of 'high
culture.' I sat next but one to the Bard and heard most of his
talk. . . ." [7] He met Andrew Lang, Spencer and Huxley, the historian Froude and Robert Browning, and also Mrs. Cashel Hoey,
cousin of a young Irishman of whom the world was soon to hear—
George Bernard Shaw. The following year he joined the Reform
Club, met Walter Pater and George Meredith, and renewed his
acquaintance with Matthew Arnold. During a visit to Scotland he
met and was impressed by the famous beauty Lillie Langtry. From
this year dates his long friendship with George du Maurier, illus-
trator of *Punch* and author of *Trilby*. He also met several important
artists including his compatriot James McNeill Whistler, Frederick
Leighton, Holman Hunt, and Samuel Laurence (who had done a
portrait of Henry James, Senior). He was certainly managing, as he
wrote William, to "feed on English minds" [8]—and at English tables:
he proudly announced to Grace Norton that he had "dined out

[7] *Letters,* I, 53.
[8] *Letters,* I, 51.

during the past winter [1878–1879] 107 times." [9] He had become quite the young lion.

The heady stuff he was imbibing stimulated but did not intoxicate. His pen was busy. In addition to several shorter works of fiction and some travel pieces, he published his second "international novel," *The American* (1877); a novella, *The Europeans* (1878)—also an international tale—a thorough revision of the early novel *Watch and Ward* (1878); and three more important "firsts": his first collection of critical essays, *French Poets and Novelists* (1878); his first critical biography, *Hawthorne* (1879); and his first best seller, *Daisy Miller* (1879)—which was published serially in 1878 and immediately pirated by two other magazines (flattering but unprofitable). All of the new works bear signs of change in their author. *The American* still gives strong evidence of the influence of Hawthornesque romance, but the biography *Hawthorne* is clearly a hail and farewell to that influence; *The Europeans* and especially *Daisy Miller* both cast a much harsher and almost unfavorable light on the general American scene; the collection of criticism by its title alone indicates the definite trend in James's interests. Most important of all these activities, however, was his beginning work on what was to be his first literary masterpiece, *The Portrait of a Lady*. James seems to have known from the outset that it would be something distinctly other than what he had done before. He wrote to his mother in March of 1878: "The story Howells is about to publish [*The Europeans*] is *by no means* the one of which I wrote you last summer that it would be to the *American* 'as wine unto water.' *That* is still in my hands; but I hope to do something with it this summer." He adds, in a tone only half jocular, the assurance that the novel will "cover you with fame." [10]

Meanwhile James had of course continued his association with the literary world of Paris and especially with the Flaubert group—"the new votaries of realism," he called them; he watched with particular interest the early flourishing of literary Naturalism under the firm note-taking hand of Émile Zola. He duly took account of the success of *L'Assommoir* in 1877, and of the confirmation of that success in the triple publication of 1880—*Nana, Le Roman expérimental,* and *Les Soirées de Médan.* He immediately wrote a review of

---

[9] *Letters,* I, 69.
[10] *The Selected Letters of Henry James,* ed. Leon Edel (New York: Farrar, Straus & Giroux, 1955), pp. 52–53.

Nana, which, while not favorable to the novel, expresses distinct admiration of Zola generally: "the system on which the series of *Les Rougons-Macquart* has been written, contains, to our sense, a great deal of solid ground. Mr. Zola's attempt is an extremely fine one; it deserves a great deal of respect and deference. . . ." [11] As though to keep pace with his growing interest in the realists and naturalists—George Eliot in England and the Flaubert circle in France—he gave explicit statement to what was already implicit in his fiction by completing his critical biography of his first master, Hawthorne—completing it, appropriately, in Paris. That little book is a tribute to Hawthorne but also a definite leave-taking from his influence: Hawthorne was a remarkable American romancer, James's thesis goes, but not enough of a realist. The volume also permits James to examine the problem posed for the American artist generally by the cultural poverty of the American scene and to suggest expatriation to Europe as a perfectly viable solution.

The Hawthorne influence is immediately replaced—it never entirely disappears—by that of George Eliot and Ivan Turgenev. In writing *The Portrait of a Lady* James drew inspiration (the novel is in no sense derivative) from *Daniel Deronda* and Turgenev's *On the Eve.* His third major novel on the "international theme"—and his last for over twenty years—*The Portrait of a Lady* was published by Macmillan in 1881. It marks the end of the first period of James's career. He returned to America in the autumn of that year, revisited Newport, spent Christmas with his family, and met the famous Oscar Wilde in Washington. But nothing would be the same again, either in his life or in his career.

Early in the new year he was stricken by the death of his mother. "She was our life, she was the house, she was the keystone of the arch. She held us all together, and without her we are scattered reeds." [12] Before the year was out his father was dead; a few months later brother Wilky followed his parents to the grave. The arch was indeed collapsing and the reeds being scattered. William had married in 1878; Emerson, the old friend of the family, had also died in 1882. Henry James's American roots were being brutally severed. The tender roots he had put down in Europe would need now to be strengthened and multiplied. Even there, however, other terminations struck him; George Eliot and Gustave Flaubert had died in 1880,

[11] *Future of the Novel,* p. 92.
[12] *The Notebooks of Henry James,* ed. F. O. Matthiessen and Kenneth B. Murdock (New York: George Braziller, Inc., 1953), p. 40.

and when James finally regained his London home in the autumn of 1883 he was met with the news that his friend and literary colleague Turgenev had reached the end of his suffering in death. The turning point could hardly be more indelibly marked. James was forty; his first masterpiece behind him signaled the end of his journeyman years. It was time to make a fresh start. James published the first collective edition of his works, in fourteen volumes, with Macmillan. If that seems an appropriate end to those early "untried years," it is an even more appropriate beginning of his middle years. On the title page of the collective edition appeared, for the first time, "by Henry James." Henry James, *Junior*, was no more.

THE EXPERIMENTAL MIDDLE YEARS

The fresh start for Henry James is marked by his return to London in the autumn of 1883, and his settling more firmly than ever before into English life—and into a new *home*. His letters during the remaining years of the eighties indicate his desire to get out of the social whirl and to find more time for his own artistic pursuits. For James seems to have been determined to be much more the professional man of letters: to continue his strict devotion to the sacred vocation of literature, but also to "succeed"—to gain the public ear (and eye) as he had not quite managed to do earlier—and to reap the consequent financial rewards. To some degree, then, his major literary undertakings of the next ten years can be seen as experiments in achieving popular success.

James had been following the progress of the group of French writers he had met in 1875, and especially that of Émile Zola. In February of 1884 he crossed the Channel to renew and strengthen his association with the "grandsons of Balzac"—moved, perhaps, by the recent loss of his friend Turgenev. He visited Zola, Goncourt, and Daudet. The inspiration of Daudet's *L'Evangéliste* was partly responsible for the new novel James was working on at this time, *The Bostonians*. In fact the precept and example of the French group generally, and the Naturalist mode in particular, form the dominant note in James's major writing of this period—both fiction and criticism. He wrote to Howells, his American colleague, praising the Flaubert group, "with its truly infernal intelligence of art, form, manner—its intense artistic life." He confessed flatly that those writers were the ones whose work he now respected, and that in spite of "their handling of unclean things, they are at least serious and honest"—which is more than he can say of the "tepid soap and water" being produced in England.[13]

But the responsible literary professional could not be content with private expressions of critical opinion, he must engage himself publicly and polemically. The chance for such engagement appeared in the form of an essay—first read as a lecture—by the English novelist Walter Besant on the art of fiction. James in turn published his own essay on "The Art of Fiction" in 1884, directing it at Besant's essay. He thus had entered a vigorous controversy, alive on both sides of the Channel, over the nature of fiction and its aims and limits. Essentially, the essay develops three main points. James begins by welcoming the opportunity to agree with Besant's claim that fiction must be given serious consideration as a fine art. The first point of note is James's emphasis on the kind of art he conceives fiction to be: like the painter, the novelist must be faithful to life as it actually appears. Thus James asserts that "the air of reality (solidity of specification) seems to me to be the supreme virtue of a novel." [14] Here he gives explicit expression to a guiding principle of his earlier essays on Scott, Dickens, Trollope, George Eliot, and Balzac (he had always admired the "palpable, provable world" of Balzac's fiction), one that had been responsible for his attraction to the Flaubert group. A second point is his demand for freedom for the artist to choose what subject he will; the critic must not prescribe the choice and he must not prejudge the work according to the subject chosen. The writer must be judged according to what he *makes of* the subject chosen; the critic's main task, then, is to attend to the treatment, the manner, in a word, the art of the work. And there must be no mean quibble about the morality—in any narrow sense —of the work: judgment of art, he insists, is an esthetic function not an ethical one (and thus he extended himself perhaps a bit further than he really wanted to go).

The third essential point is a reflection on the implications of the second: James insists that the novel be regarded as an organic whole with every part a functioning contributor to the achieving of the novel's ultimate expression. "A novel is a living thing, all one and continuous, like any other organism," he claims.[15] Implicit in this claim is the role of the author in relation to his work: he must re-

---

[13] *Letters*, I, 104–105.
[14] *Future of the Novel*, p. 14.
[15] *Future of the Novel*, p. 15.

main outside, not appear within it to explain or plead or point the moral—or otherwise confess to the novel's imperfection, its lack of self-sufficiency. Behind all three major points lies James's experience of the "grandsons of Balzac": their attitudes are very similar to those expressed in the essay, and on one or two occasions the very language of "The Art of Fiction" echoes that of Zola and Flaubert.

The reply to Besant provoked in its turn a response from Robert Louis Stevenson, "A Humble Remonstrance," which gently took James to task for presenting a somewhat unbalanced view. James was quick to reply to Stevenson by letter, admitting the justice of the remonstrance, confessing that "The Art of Fiction" presented but half of what he had to say. This was something of an exaggeration, but a graceful gesture that was the beginning of a new friendship (the story of which is nicely told in Janet Adam Smith's *A Literary Friendship*).

Soon after, James finished and published almost simultaneously the first two novels of his middle period—*The Bostonians* and *The Princess Casamassima* (1886). The former, his only major novel that is purely American, is a humorous satire of certain aspects of American life—the clamor for cheap publicity, faddish interest in any sort of "reform" movement, and popular fascination with mesmerists, inspirational speakers, and the like. The latter is purely European and deals with the topical subject of social revolution and international anarchy. Both novels are attentive, unusually so for James, to ample realistic detail and offer accurate descriptions of familiar places and institutions of the time. Furthermore, these two together with the third of the decade, *The Tragic Muse*—a novel of politics, art, and the theater—are examples of James's attempt to adapt to his own uses the mode of literary Naturalism championed by Zola. In some striking ways all three are "experimental novels" of Zolaesque type. Much emphasis is given to the influence of heredity and to the matching or directly contrasting influence of environment as determining the fate of the principal characters of the novels. They are, finally, closer in tone and attitude to the fiction of Alphonse Daudet than to the fiction of Zola: both James and Daudet were to a degree following the precepts of Zola.

James's esthetic interest in the theory and practice of his French contemporaries was reinforced by his practical and professional interest in their popularity. Popular success meant tangible reward—money in the bank—and James had reason to be sensitive to that attraction. His sister, Alice, had followed him to England late in

1884—the last scattering of the reeds; her increasing illness made increasing fraternal demands, and not less financial demands. He was hopeful that the two novels of 1886, of which he thought highly, would do well. But even while *The Bostonians* was beginning its serial run, fate dealt him an ironic blow: one of his principal publishers, James R. Osgood, went bankrupt. He was to publish the novel, but when the tangle cleared, *The Bostonians* brought James only a fraction of the amount he had contracted for with Osgood. (As he might have foreseen, the novel was roughly handled by American reviewers!) *The Princess Casamassima* did not fare measurably better. James wrote despondently to Howells that those two books from which he had expected so much benefit had actually done him harm, had "reduced the desire, and demand, for my productions to zero." He adds that for the past while he has been writing "a number of good short things." [16]

During the latter half of the eighties James did indeed write quite a number of good tales—international stories like "Lady Barberina," *The Siege of London,* and "A Modern Warning," and stories of writers and artists like "The Author of 'Beltraffio' " and "The Lesson of the Master"—as well as his usual quota of critical essays and reviews. A combination of factors would persuade him to forsake the novel form and restrict his fiction to the shorter genre after completion of *The Tragic Muse.* The disappointing reception of *The Bostonians* and *The Princess Casamassima* of course helped influence that decision; and perhaps the brilliant young Maupassant's visit to him in London in 1886 encouraged James to devote more energy to exploring the possibilities of the shorter form. (He published an important essay on Maupassant in 1888). But certainly the crucial event was the invitation extended him to prepare a dramatized version of *The American* for production by Edward Compton's company. He had only to finish his "last long novel," *The Tragic Muse,* and then he could avail himself of this opportunity to escape from the depressing life of the novelist into the brave new world of the theater with its immediate and broad publicity and its generous financial rewards: a blessed release.

This is not to suggest that the eighties were years of unrelieved bleakness for James. They were years in which he made new and lasting friendships—with Alphonse Daudet, Stevenson, and the painter John Singer Sargent, with Edmund Gosse, George du

---

[16] *Letters,* I, 135.

Maurier, Paul Bourget, and the Humphry Wards. One friendship in particular stands out peculiarly from the others, for it was the one possibly romantic attachment that James formed during his middle years: it involved Constance Fenimore Woolson, a minor American novelist three years his senior, the grandniece of James Fenimore Cooper. Her relationship with the severely celibate Henry James could hardly have been much more than good friendship; yet it was evidently rather a special kind of friendship at that.

They met first in Europe in 1879, but their relationship did not begin its gentle blossoming until the autumn of 1883. There were occasional meetings during the next few years—evenings at the theater, coincident visits to Dover, a journey together from Salisbury to Stonehenge. The fullest flowering occurred in 1887, when they were in close touch as near neighbors in Florence. The following spring found them under the same roof in a villa at Bellosguardo—though in separate apartments. This "intimacy" lasted but a few weeks: Henry James returned to London alone that summer. Although they were never quite so close again, they did see each other infrequently during the next eight years, or until Fenimore's shocking death was reported to James from Venice.

Meantime, Henry James was contemplating with eager anticipation the opportunity to go to work on Edward Compton's invitation to turn *The American* into a play. Now, in addition to its other various attractions, that invitation would give James the chance to realize what had been "the most cherished of all my projects." [17] If it was the most cherished it was also very nearly the earliest. In *A Small Boy and Others*, he recorded his great excitement over theater-going as a youngster in New York. And it is a genial coincidence that the earliest letter we have from James's pen —from one small American to another—expresses his precocious interest in matters theatrical: "As I heard you were going to try to turn the club into a Theatre. And I was asked w'ether I wanted to belong here is my answer. I would like very much to belong. Yours truly H. James." [18]

James had published three plays before he was thirty; but the theater itself did not beckon overtly until 1881, when he was asked to dramatize his popular *Daisy Miller* for the Madison Square Theatre. What that meant to him he confided in his Notebooks: the

[17] *Notebooks,* p. 37.
[18] To Edgar Van Winkle, 1854; *Selected Letters,* p. 113.

long-awaited opportunity—"None has given me brighter hopes—
none has given me sweeter emotions. . . . and I ache with trying to
settle down at last to a sustained attempt in this direction." [19] But
his bright hopes were dashed by this, the first of a series of disappointments that he was to meet with in the theater. The play was
rejected. He published the text in 1883, however; and the following
year entertained a request from the actor Lawrence Barrett to
dramatize *The Portrait of a Lady.* James did not comply, but was
careful not to discourage future requests from Barrett: "I should
probably be prepared to write you a play [next year]," he replied,
"on the chance that if you *should* like it, it would open the door to
my acquiring a goodish sum of money." [20]

If there seems to have been uncertainty in James's attitude—he
would not say yes, but he would not say no—there were good reasons
for it. He knew the theater; he had been from the first an inveterate
theater-goer; he could call not only Fanny Kemble but Coquelin,
Pauline Viardot, and Julia Bartet his friends. And he was keenly
critical of the contemporary stage; he admired especially the well-
made plays of Sardou, Scribe, Dumas fils, and Émile Augier—yet
even they failed to satisfy his strict requirements. His critical observations indicate that his attitude was not simply that of an enlightened spectator but rather that of a colleague, a fellow practitioner, even of a competitor. If he knew their limitations—he said
of the French dramatists that he had them "in my pocket" [21]—
he understood how to do as well as they, if not better.

Yet at the same time he was most severely critical of the theater
itself, of the conditions to which a playwright must submit—the
demands of managers, directors, and actors, and worst of all the
demands of an overfed, hurried, squeezed-together and insufficiently
enlightened public: "the vulgarity, the brutality, the baseness of the
condition of the English-speaking theatre today," [22] he phrased it
in his Notebooks. How could he not hesitate, not doubt himself for
his eagerness to try his hand at this unholy trade; and how could
he not question most astringently his own motives—especially his
unabashed quest for lucre?

The problem plagued him and is reflected in much of the fiction

[19] *Notebooks,* p. 37.
[20] Quoted in *The Complete Plays of Henry James,* ed. Leon Edel (Philadelphia: J. B. Lippincott Company, 1949), p. 44.
[21] *Notebooks,* p. 38.
[22] *Notebooks,* p. 99.

he wrote during this period of dubious endeavor and questionable attempt. The "last long novel" itself (*The Tragic Muse*) addresses this plaguey problem quite directly. Miram Rooth, the rising young actress in the novel, suffers variously from the conditions of the theater as James outlined them in his Notebook; and it is significant that her principal difficulty is one that James himself was acutely aware of facing. She is caught by the need to keep repeating her "hit" performances to a packed house—to reap the financial rewards; yet she is driven by her desire to try other plays, to experiment, to develop herself as an artist. The distinct threat of prostitution thus hangs over her head; and she might well repeat James's grim words to himself in his Notebook:

Of art or fame *il est maintenant fort peu question:* I simply *must* try, and try seriously, to produce half a dozen . . . plays for the sake of my pocket, my material future. Of how little money the novel makes for me I needn't discourse here.[23]

For "novel" Miriam might substitute "a new play" or "a demanding role" or "a fresh interpretation." Her problem is reflected in the career of Nick Dormer, a promising young politician who wishes to paint. Like Miriam, he is caught between the public demand, with its attendant material reward, and his personal impulse to be an artist. *The Tragic Muse* was in some way a wish-fulfilling exercise for James: the mysterious, angelic, esthetic Gabriel Nash assures Nick that *being* an artist is all that matters, that what he specifically *does* is of secondary importance.

James's dubiousness about his theatrical venture is similarly reflected in the large number of stories about artists that he wrote during the period. They deal in various ways with the artist's difficulty in standing up to the demands of his public—to produce often and give them what they want. For James dearly needed some satisfactory explanation and justification of what he was doing. In his Notebooks he offered himself the explanation that the money he earned from writing for the stage would afford him greater leisure for "one's general artistic life" and especially "for 'real literature' "—his blessed work of fiction.[24] The short stories about writers and artists examine and test that explanation.

So he did *The American* for Compton. It was finished and in

[23] *Notebooks,* p. 99.
[24] *Notebooks,* p. 99.

Compton's hands by the spring of 1890, and James went off to Europe—mainly to Italy. His holiday was interrupted, however, by news that Alice was suddenly much more seriously ill. He hurried home and had her moved up to London from Leamington, where she and her companion had been living for the past couple of years. Cancer was diagnosed and her eventual demise accurately forecast. James's concern was now equally divided between his sister, dying, and his play, about to be born.

The American had its first night on January 3, 1891, with Compton as Christopher Newman and his wife as Claire de Cintré. It was quite a thumping success. It continued to do well in the provinces and in Scotland and Ireland. That did not assure its success in London, however, and James was anxious to put it to that test. Some few days after the play's opening, James met the young American actress Elizabeth Robins; and before the month was over he saw her play Nora in *A Doll's House*—his first experience with the newly translated Ibsen—and shortly after in the title role in *Hedda Gabler*. He was sufficiently impressed to persuade Compton to get Miss Robins to play the role of Claire in the London production. Mrs. Compton was expecting a child and would be pleased to relinquish the role; and her sister, Kate Bateman, would come out of retirement to play Claire's mother, the Marquise de Bellegarde.

With these changes, *The American* was set for its London debut in the refurbished Opera Comique Theatre in late September of 1891. William was with his brother on opening night, as he had hurried across from America to say his adieux to the rapidly failing Alice, who died the next March.

The critics were not favorably impressed with James's first dramatic offering in London. They found that Miss Robins could not handle the quiet Claire as well as she had the vigorous and vibrant heroines of Ibsen; and James had been too careful not to make his play "too good"—strengthening the melodramatic strain that darkens the novel and simplifying the characters almost to caricature. It ran for seventy performances but "made no money," as James informed William.

Yet he persisted, writing plays for Sir John Hare, for Ada Rehan and Augustin Daly, none of which was produced. He took time out to visit Paul Bourget and his bride in Siena; Bourget had been for some time an admiring disciple of James and had dedicated his novel *Cruelle Enigme* to him. James went on to Venice to visit with Katherine Bronson and the amazing Mrs. Jack—Isabella Gardner, a truly Jamesian international heroine, the collector (with Bernard Berenson's aid) of the treasures of the Gardner Museum. Then in Switzerland he visited with William and his family; and finally, the following year, he spent some time with the ailing Daudet. He was back in London in time for the opening of Pinero's *The Second Mrs. Tanqueray*, and was impressed both by the play and with the acting of George Alexander. In Alexander, James felt, he had found a man who could give adequate treatment to a serious play of his own. He offered Alexander his new play *Guy Domville*.

Guy Domville was indeed a serious play, and represented an artistic advance on what James had done earlier. Any disappointment in its career would be bound to affect its author deeply. Disappointments began at once. There was an initial skirmish with Alexander over terms—not so serious as that with Daly, which resulted in James's withdrawing his play *Disengaged*; yet that was not all: the play was ready for rehearsal in the autumn of 1893, but Alexander had a prior commitment that kept *Guy Domville* from going into rehearsal until December 1894.

In January of 1894 James got news of Miss Woolson's death in Venice, just a year after the death of his old friend Fanny Kemble in London. Again he prepared to go to the funeral of a lost loved one; but when he then learned the nature of Fenimore's death he changed his plans—she had commited suicide. Leon Edel, James's biographer, is persuaded that a kind of crisis had been reached in the relationship of James and Fenimore in 1892, perhaps precipitated by the death of his sister, Alice: it seems he felt himself being drawn into an intimacy he could not accept. An annual visit to her in Italy was all he would henceforth permit himself. With her suicide, some pang of guilt may have struck James. Had he played John Marcher to Fenimore's May Bartram—had his short story "The Beast in the Jungle" acted itself out already in his own life? In any case, he could not bring himself to travel to Venice to help clear up Fenimore's effects until the end of March.

To the peculiar grief of Miss Woolson's death was added, later that year, the news of Robert Louis Stevenson's death in far-off Samoa, which reached James just as rehearsal was beginning on his new play. The horizon must have seemed clouded to him as he faced the opening of *Guy Domville* on January 5, 1895, at St. James's Theatre in London.

The whole of the rather grisly story of the fate of *Guy Domville* is admirably told by Leon Edel in his introduction to *The Complete Plays of Henry James*. Briefly, Alexander had provoked some animos-

ity by his slighting a young actress, and the occasion of his opening in
a new play was chosen as the moment for retribution. A band of
London "roughs," planted in the gallery, began with the opening of
the second act to harass the actors with uncomplimentary interpola-
tions and general rowdyism. The play struggled to the final curtain,
but had by then been reduced to something of a fiasco. The angered
Alexander permitted the unwary author to face a riled and unruly
audience for a curtain call. James had sought to escape the tension of
opening night at a nearby production of Wilde's *An Ideal Husband*
and had returned just at the closing curtain. In truth, the reception
was mixed, but James noticed only the hoots and jeers of the gallery
It was a shocking experience for him and had much to do with his
decision to bid the theater a not too fond adieu.

Certain discerning critics permitted *Guy Domville* a *succès d'es-
time*: H. G. Wells, A. B. Walkley, Arnold Bennett, and George
Bernard Shaw all wrote favorable reviews. Nevertheless, after the
play's four-week run, James's theatrical experiment was ended. A
friendly inquiry from the actress Ellen Terry persuaded James to
write a play for her, *Summersoft,* before the end of the year; and
while she apparently liked the play, she never used it.

Before the short month of the run of *Guy Domville* was ended,
indeed, James had made his decision and committed it to his Notebook:

> I take up my *own* old pen again—the pen of all my old unforgettable
> efforts and sacred struggles. To myself—today—I need say no more.
> Large and full and high the future still opens. It is now indeed that
> I may do the work of my life. And I will.[25]

His own old pen had, of course, never been entirely abandoned, as the
number of short stories published during the dramatic years amply
testifies. During spare moments amid the hurry of his less sacred
struggles with the "unspeakable theatric form," he was able to dip
that pen "into the *other* ink—the sacred fluid of fiction." In mid-
1893 he found a moment to cherish that blessed resource: "nothing is
so soothing as to remember that literature sits patient at my door,
and that I have only to lift the latch to let in the exquisite little form
that is, after all, nearest to my heart and with which I am so far
from having done." [26]

[25] *Notebooks*, p. 179.
[26] *Notebooks*, pp. 133–134.

The first task he set to his old pen was the writing of a short story, "The Next Time." The idea for it had come to him and been duly set down in his Notebook even while *Guy Domville* was still playing. It is the story of a writer who needs to write for money but can never write badly enough to catch on with the public taste: Ray Limbert's talent tries "to 'meet' the vulgar need, to violate his intrinsic conditions, to make, as it were, a sow's ear out of a silk purse." Of course Ray Limbert, like the playwright Henry James, cannot manage to do it: "It's all of no use—it's always 'too subtle,' always too fine—never, never vulgar enough." [27] The key phrase in the note, James recovered from a letter to William explaining *Domville*'s failure on opening night: "I tried so to meet them! But you can't make a sow's ear out of a silk purse." [28] James would, then, keep henceforth to the silk purse, the old pen, the sacred fluid.

James's theatrical experiment may have been a failure, but it was not absolutely unfruitful: his work in the dramatic mode proved to be a most useful experience. He made the nice distinction between the theater and the drama in a rather hurried letter written on New Year's Eve, 1894, the night of the dress rehearsal of *Domville:* "I may have been meant for the Drama—God knows!—but I certainly wasn't meant for the Theatre." [29] Just how valuable the dramatic training had been, James was soon to discover. But at the moment of turning to his own old pen again, he must have been tremendously depressed, at a spiritual nadir. Once again, and now approaching his fifty-second birthday, he was faced with the need to make yet another fresh beginning.

THE MAJOR PHASE

Shortly after the collapse of *Guy Domville* James paid a visit to his friend the Archbishop of Canterbury at Addington. James's state of mind at that moment is graphically represented in a comment of his that A. C. Benson, one of the Archbishop's sons, recorded: "hitherto he had seemed to himself to have been struggling in some dim water-world, bewildered and hampered by the crystal medium, and that he had suddenly got his head above the surface, with a

[27] *Notebooks,* p. 180.
[28] *Letters,* I, 229.
[29] *Letters,* I, 226.

new perspective and an unimpended vision." [30] If that is not an image
of death and rebirth, it is certainly expressive of a successful recovery from dire difficulties—the happy emerging, cleansed and re-
freshed, after a plunge into the depths. During the preceding year
of struggle, James had often been near despair, and thoughts of
death constantly preoccupied him—death as a theme runs through
the entries in his Notebooks. One note considers the cases in which
consciousness may survive death:

> In what cases *may* the consciousness be said to survive—so that
> the man is the spectator of his own tragedy? In the cases of defeat,
> of failure, of subjection, of sacrifice to other bribes or other con-
> siderations. [31]

James knew such cases well—and at firsthand. Subsequent Notebook entries—for "The Death of the Lion," "The Altar of the Dead,"
and *The Wings of the Dove*—examine ideas for stories that asso-
ciate death with the failure of love: either love is unable to sustain
actual life, or love is possible only after a more or less sacrificial death.
The biographical impulse in this is clear enough: James's recent
struggle has threatened to end in his "death" as an artist through
failure to win his public's love, the death-blow being struck finally
by the brutal rejection, as he felt it, of his plays.

Yet the *real* Henry James was as much alive as ever—perhaps
even more alive, so to speak, as a result of the "death" of the Henry
James who had been fondly wooing the bitch goddess. The real artist
was now free to resume his own old pen and start his artistic life
anew. The idea of fresh beginnings is coincidentally reflected in
James's choice of principal characters for his immediately subsequent stories: they are all children—little Effie in *The Other House;*
Maisie, the heroine of *What Maisie Knew;* Miles and Flora, the
haunted children of *The Turn of the Screw;* Nanda Brookenham of
The Awkward Age. (James had in fact picked up the germ for the
story of *The Turn of the Screw* from the Archbishop of Canterbury
during the visit mentioned above.) While the presence of these
youngsters in his fiction seems to reflect the beginning of a new
phase, the intrigues in which they are involved assure us that some-

[30] *Memories and Friends* (New York and London: G. P. Putnam's Sons,
1924), p. 216.
[31] *Notebooks*, p. 144; see also pp. 183–184.

thing of the old James persists: the imagination of disaster is as active as it ever was. Effie Bream is murdered, as she is the representative of a selfish love and seems to stand in the way of the fulfillment of another love; Miles and Flora are haunted by the spectres of corrupting adults and suffer further under the stifling "protection" of the strange possessive love of their governess; what Maisie knew was the bizarre unhappiness that resulted from her parents' separation and subsequent partnerships that volleyed her about in their love-matches; and Nanda, somewhat older, knew far more than Maisie, far more than a young Victorian girl ought to have had to know about the limp morality of her family and her mother's friends, and was spoiled by her precocious knowledge of the ways of the world and by her severely moral judgment of her own sophistication.

The beginning was made, and the new perspective and unimpeded vision are to be seen most brilliantly in James's advances in the development of narrative technique. With the novels and tales of the closing years of the nineteenth century James was clearly embarking on the period of his greatest literary production—the "major phase," as F. O. Matthiessen so well termed it. The turn of the century finds him reaching the peak of his powers; it was then, indeed, that he accomplished "the work of my life," as he had foretold.

James escaped England in the spring of 1895 and spent a comparatively carefree month in Ireland. He was back in England to greet Daudet, who had managed once more to make the journey; and he took him to visit George Meredith at Box Hill. Much of the time he spent industriously at his desk at 34 De Vere Gardens. He published two volumes of short stories written during these trying years, stories devoted largely to the theme of the writer's dilemma; the volumes bore the significant titles *Terminations* (1895) and *Embarrassments* (1896). He was also then preparing two longer pieces of fiction, *The Other House* (1896) and *The Spoils of Poynton* (1897), which he might well have published under the joint title of *Compensations;* for while the traumatic effect of his failure in the theater was still active, he nevertheless recognized that he had gained certain valuable lessons from his brief skirmish with the theater— certain definite compensations. Not only was he able to salvage as stories some of his unproduced writing for the stage—*The Other House* and *Summersoft,* which became "Covering End" (1898)— but he learned the value of *dramatic* preparation of his material for fiction according to what he called "the divine principle of the Scenario." Thus, in turning over the germinal idea for *The Golden Bowl* James wrote in his Notebooks (February 1895):

> Compensations and solutions seem to stand there with open arms for me. . . . Has a *part* of all this wasted passion and squandered time (of the last 5 years) been simply the precious lesson . . . *of the singular value for a narrative plan too* of the . . . divine principle of the Scenario . . . a key that, working in the same *general* way fits the complicated chambers of *both* the dramatic and the narrative lock . . . ?[32]

Throughout the copious notes for *The Spoils of Poynton* James refers to the same lesson, of the mastery of statement, "of the art and secret of it, of expression, of the sacred mystery of structure."[33] And repeatedly he admonishes himself in his notes to "Dramatize!" Finally, of course, there is the unmistakable evidence of his work itself, the increasingly dramatic aspect of his subsequent fiction.

In the summer of 1896 James took himself away from his busy desk in London for a holiday on the Sussex coast. That proved to be one of the happy turning points in James's life, for it led to his establishing at last a permanent home for himself on English soil. He had gone to Point Hill, Playden, Rye, and found it so delightful that he prolonged his holiday another two months, moving then to the vicarage at Rye. Not only was he attracted by the mild and mellow Sussex countryside and the lovely old town of Rye, but particularly by a charming dwelling called Lamb House. It was named after the family that built and occupied it for many years, the Lamb family, and who had filled the office of Mayor of Rye for a good number of years during the eighteenth century. It boasted a "King's Room," after George I, who shipwrecked on the Channel coast near Rye, came ashore and spent the night in the Mayor's house. James later learned by chance that the house had fallen vacant, and by September of the following year had signed a lease for Lamb House for twenty-one years (at the sum of £2.000). In a letter to William's wife, Henry crows jubilantly over his acquisition:

> I will try to have a photograph taken of the pleasant little old-world town-angle into which its nice old red-bricked front, its high old

[32] *Notebooks*, p. 188.
[33] *Notebooks*, p. 208.

Georgian doorway and a most delightful little old architectural garden-house, perched alongside of it on its high brick garden wall . . . "compose" . . . about an acre of garden and lawn, all shut in by the peaceful old red wall aforesaid, in which the most flourishing old espaliers, apricots, pears, plums and figs, assiduously grow.[34]

James was settled in by July of 1898, and soon was assured that Lamb House was all he had hoped for. The years in Rye promised to be the happiest of his life. He was now definitely rooted, a householder, and an active (so to speak) participating member of the community of Rye. He was able to play the host at Lamb House to numerous guests as he had never quite been able to do before—to Edmund Gosse, Jonathan Sturges, A. C. Benson, Hugh Walpole, Howard Sturgis, Howells, T. S. Perry, Edith Wharton, Mrs. Humphry Ward, and to his brother William and his family. He was fortunate also in his neighbors in the general area of the Cinque Ports: Joseph Conrad, H. G. Wells, poor Stephen Crane, and others figured largely in James's Lamb House days—and their association was by no means always exclusively "literary." There was, for example, Crane's Christmas play written for the entertainment of his neighbors at the village of Brede, according to this plan that Crane sketched: "I have hit upon a plan of making the programmes choice by printing thereon a terrible list of authors of the comedy and to that end I have asked Henry James, Joseph Conrad, A. E. W. Mason, H. G. Wells, Edwin Pugh, George Gissing, Rider Haggard and yourself [Marriot-Watson] to write a mere word—any word 'it,' 'they,' 'you,'—any word and thus identify themselves with this crime" (from Crane's *Letters*, ed. R. W. Stallman and Lillian Gilkes, New York University Press, 1960, p. 243). The wonderful crime was duly committed in December of 1899, in the Brede schoolhouse. In addition to sharing in such shenanigans as that, James also was attendant at local bazaars and flower-shows; he was a member of the local golf club—although he never touched a niblick in his life—and a supporter of the local cricketers—although he spent most of the matches in the tea-tent, supporting the supporters rather than the players.

Life was good at Rye: it seemed to offer James the perfect combination of the social and the private that he had always sought. His mornings were kept quite strictly for his writing; his afternoons were free for his guests and neighbors and for his community interests. To

[34] *Letters*, I, 265–266.

match this pleasant new arrangement he also began a new method of literary creation and composition: he turned from writing to dictating his work to a typist. He had first had recourse to the typewriter some time late in 1896 or early in 1897, because of a combination of rheumatism and fatigue; it became a fixed practice during the Lamb House years. While his typed letters are at first prefaced with elaborate apologies for his "Remingtonese," he was soon quite at home with the machine; he found, he explained, that this method of oral composition to the accompaniment of the mechanical click—and the click of the Remington, he insisted, was the most conducive to composition!—was the most satisfactory he had ever employed. So content was he with this new arrangement in his life that with the exception of one four-month interval in 1899, he did not set foot out of England until his visit to America in 1904.

One adjustment to his way of life he did make: he had originally intended to live the year round at Rye, but he was to find the winters left him more isolated than he could accept. The adjustment was to spend one half of the year, May to October, in Lamb House and the other half up in London, first in his old apartment at 34 De Vere Gardens but later in a set of rooms in the Reform Club.

Meanwhile he was busy writing and seeing works through the press. There were critical pieces on George Sand, Howells, and Stevenson, and two significant essays on "The American Novel" and "The New Novel." His two major novels, *What Maisie Knew* and *The Awkward Age*, represent important extended experiments in narrative technique—particularly in narrative focus, or "point of view." In 1901 he developed the technique further in *The Sacred Fount*. These technical experiments were to bear rich fruit in the three great novels that then followed in quick succession. He also produced a large number of short stories, many of which were collected in *The Soft Side* (1900) and *The Better Sort* (1903), and his substantial biography of *William Wetmore Story and His Friends* (1903).

Of course the most outstanding feature of this the last period of James's career was his impressive production of three novels in three successive years—*The Wings of the Dove* (1902), *The Ambassadors* (1903), and *The Golden Bowl* (1904). At the very height of his artistic power he turned again to the international theme for the substance of these novels. *The Wings of the Dove* recounts the bittersweet story of Milly Theale, the wealthy American girl, whose very name recalls the long dead Minny Temple, James's one true love, and her brief but finally fruitful life in Europe and especially in Italy—where Henry and Minny had planned to meet. *The Ambassadors* is a tale of Americans in Paris and hence in some sense a sequel to the earlier *The American;* James would always consider this his best work—and with justification, for it represents his technical best combined with his most typical subject. *The Golden Bowl,* the last of the three, again raises the question of the possibility of successful marriage between the fresh, new American girl and the European aristocrat of long tradition and ancestry. This would be his last major novel, and it is supremely appropriate that in it James managed to effect the successful compromise toward which all his international fiction had from the first been yearning: the antinomies are reconciled and the American fruitfully weds her European. If *The Golden Bowl* is not his "best, 'all round,'" it nevertheless is his most adult novel in the full maturity of its moral attitude.

While *The Ambassadors* was running serially in the *North American Review,* James was entertaining the idea of arranging a revised and definitive edition of his fiction to be published by Scribner. There was the added excitement of the visit to his homeland, after more than twenty years of uninterrupted absence, in connection with the arrangement. As the idea came closer to realization there was further added the interest and attraction (at least financial) of an American lecture tour. James sailed in August of 1904.

The affair was duly settled with Scribner, including a rather odd stipulation of James's that the edition (the New York Edition, it has come to be called) run to twenty-three volumes—no more and no fewer. The explanation of this strange stipulation is simply that James wanted his edition to emulate the edition of Balzac's works, which he knew, and which had consisted of twenty-three plum-colored volumes. It is hardly coincidental that for his lecture tour James chose "The Lesson of Balzac" as one of the two subjects he would lecture on—the other was "The Question of Our Speech." In the Balzac lecture James pays a glowing tribute to the French writer, calling him "the father of us all"—all us novelists—and "the greatest master."

I speak of him, and can only speak, as a man of his own craft, an emulous fellow-worker, who has learned from him more of the engaging mystery of fiction than from any one else, and who is conscious of so large a debt to repay that it has had positively to be discharged in installments; as if one could never have at once all the required cash in hand.[35]

The lecture tour took James down to Florida, across to California, into the Midwest, and even up into Canada. He got a broad view of his extensive and varied homeland. He was indeed impressed, but not favorably: "interesting, formidable, fearsome and fatiguing, and much more difficult to see and deal with in any extended and various way than I supposed," he would write in 1906; "an immense impression of material and political power; but almost cruelly charmless, in effect, and calculated to make one crouch, ever afterwards, as cravenly as possible, at Lamb House, Rye."[36] So he welcomed the return, at the end of the summer of 1905, to his dear old haven of Lamb House. There he set to work revising his early novels and tales and writing the eighteen wonderful prefaces that would introduce his fiction in the New York Edition. He also began to publish various travel pieces based on his American experience.

Except for a brief vacation in London, James stuck to his task down in Sussex. In 1907 *The American Scene,* the impressions from his recent tour, and the first volumes of the New York Edition appeared. Unfortunately he was not able to fit everything he wished to include into the prescribed twenty-three volumes, and the edition spilled over into a twenty-fourth. That was a minor concern, however, compared to the lukewarm reception accorded the first volumes of the Edition, of which he had been unusually hopeful.

Two other ventures of 1907 drew James away from his own old pen. He somehow managed to agree to participate in a bizarre plan sketched out by Elizabeth Jordan, lady editor of *Harper's Bazaar:* she would publish a novel written jointly by twelve authors, each contributing a chapter, to be called (with some unintentional irony) *The Whole Family.* Seemingly, this would be the last sort of thing James would care to have any truck with; he was possibly stunned with the monstrosity of the idea. But he did it, fussing constantly in letters over how on earth he was to make his chapter fit in after what was to precede it and over how well the chapter following would pick up and develop the leads he had provided in his, "The Married Son." And fuss he might: except for William Dean Howells, James's company in the creation of *The Whole Family* was a collection of distinctly lesser talents—largely lady writers with three or four

[35] *Future of the Novel,* p. 104.
[36] *Letters,* II, 48.

names, as was the vogue. More sane and satisfying was meeting the request of Johnston Forbes-Robertson for a play. James accordingly reopened his career as a playwright.

Forbes-Robertson had read James's short story "Covering End" and in 1899 had broached with him the question of dramatizing it; he undoubtedly saw dramatic possibilities in the story, which is not surprising since James had developed the story from *Summersoft,* the play he had given to Ellen Terry. James had refused then, but he accepted now and reconverted the story into the play *The High Bid.* It ran in the provinces during 1908 and briefly in London early in 1909, where it played to good houses and enjoyed a favorable press. James had clearly benefited from his theatrical experience of a decade earlier, and also from his intimate acquaintance with the work of Ibsen. He had been an Ibsenite supporter in the battle that raged in the London theaters over the Norwegian's striking drama, and he had written several appreciative essays on Ibsen during the nineties.

James dramatized two other stories of the nineties: "Owen Windgrave" became *The Saloon* and the novel *The Other House* became an Ibsenesque psychological shocker. The Irishman Herbert Trench was to include *The Other House* in his repertory for the Haymarket, but his plans fell through. Another opportunity came, however, in the invitation to contribute to Charles Frohman's repertory: James would be in the impressive company of Shaw, Galsworthy, Barrie, and Granville-Barker. Here were artists whom he could respect and at whose side he willingly took his stand against the stifling effect of British censorship of plays. He set to work on *The Outcry* in the autumn of 1909 and finished a final draft before Christmas. Then he faced the anguish of rewriting, cutting, casting, and finally rehearsals in the spring of the new year. It was depressing, exhaustive work for him, but promised to be worthwhile. His hopes were cruelly dashed, yet again, when the death of Edward VII in May meant the collapse of Frohman's venture. James salvaged *The Outcry* and published it revised as a novel in 1911, when his *The Saloon* was produced anticlimactically in London. But his work, dramatic and otherwise, was essentially behind him. The end had begun.

During the winter of 1908–1909 James had been plagued with an "ominous cardiac crisis,"[37] as he wrote to Edith Wharton; and much of 1909 was a slow but apparently sure recovery. The anxiety of

[37] *Letters,* II, 124.

preparing *The Outcry* combined with the unambiguous reports of the
public failure of his New York Edition helped to bring on another
collapse—part physical and part "nervous." Most of 1910 was, he
said, "a perfect Hell of a Time." [38] He gratefully anticipated the
visit of his brother William and his wife, who planned to come over
from America for William's health. On their arrival, however, it was
apparent to Henry that William's state of health was even more
precarious than his own. By June he had planned to return with
William and Alice to America. Just as Henry was beginning to rally
they received the news that their remaining younger brother, Robert-
son, had died. By the time they reached America, in August, William was gravely ill; he died within a week.

Henry decided to stay on in America until the next autumn. And
he received gratifying news of especial recognition: he was offered
honorary degrees both by Harvard University and by Oxford University. The Harvard degree was conferred before he left; the Oxford degree, the next year. When he regained Lamb House in September 1911, he began work on a project suggested to him by William's widow, that he write a biographical study of the family—and
principally of William. Thus he began *A Small Boy and Others,* soon
to be followed by *Notes of a Son and Brother;* and as he cast his
memory far back and began to recover those earliest years, the
volumes developed into richly anecdotal *auto*biographical reminiscences. He seldom strayed far from Lamb House, except for the
particular pleasure of a leisurely stroll down to the Channel shore;
and he devoted what strength he had to his writing and his occasional visitors—and always, of course, to his correspondence (difficult as it had become for him to sustain it), and especially with the
admiring young men who constituted a veritable discipleship to
"the Master": Hugh Walpole, Percy Lubbock, Geoffrey Keynes,
Howard Sturgis, H. G. Wells—the Judas of the group—and others.

He suffered another painful attack late in the summer of 1912,
and decided he must move into convenient quarters in London; he
took a small flat, 21 Carlyle Mansions, in Cheyne Walk on the
Chelsea embankment, which would be his last home. He was able to
finish the critical pieces that make up *Notes on Novelists* (1914) and
to begin work on another American novel; but this novel and a third
volume of reminiscences, *The Middle Years,* would be left unfinished,
and he was to complete very little more of any significance.

---

[38] *Letters,* II, 161–162.

James's seventieth birthday brought him generous recognition from nearly three hundred of the most important figures of the day; the celebrations included an arrangement for John Singer Sargent to paint James's portrait—now hanging in the National Portrait Gallery in London. The following year, however, he was stricken by one of the harshest blows he had had to face in his life—the outbreak of World War I. He was pained by the rape of Belgium and the suffering of France. He wrote to Edith Wharton from Lamb House, "we look inconceivably off across the blue channel, the lovely rim, toward the nearness of the horrors that are in perpetration just beyond." [39] He spent little of that time down in Rye, however, largely because he felt there was a good deal he could do for the war effort in London, but partly because as an alien his freedom to travel down to the Channel coast was severely restricted and closely supervised. In London James busied himself with visiting wounded troops in St. Bartholomew's Hospital and with charitable work among the Belgian refugees in the center in Chelsea; he also made generous contributions to the American volunteer motor-ambulance corps in France.

His motivation for these exertions is perfectly understandable, but a letter he wrote during the first months of the war casts an additional light on the matter: the "lacerations of France and the martyrdoms of Belgium" leave, he writes,

> small freedom of mind for general talk, it presses all the while, with every throb of consciousness; and if during the first days I felt in the air the recall of the Civil War shocks and anxieties, and hurryings and doings, of 1861, etc., the pressure in question has already become a much nearer and bigger thing, and a more formidable and tragic one, than anything we of the North in those years had to face.[40]

To that he adds, "I didn't mean to go into these historical parallels," but the fact that the parallels so readily suggested themselves to him encourages us to recognize that James was eager to grasp this opportunity for "service"—as a kind of personal compensation for his "failure" of the earlier time. Another kind of compensation was involved in his eagerness to make what contribution he could: the shame of nationality at America's failure to enter the conflict immediately on the side of the Allies.

[39] *Letters*, II, 391–392.
[40] *Letters*, II, 401.

The war touched him in quite personal ways as well: Burgess Noakes, who had been in James's service at Lamb House since his early teens and had accompanied him to America as his valet, had enlisted; and James showered on him what paternal care and advice he could. Then one of the charming and promising young men of the Cambridge group of admirers, the poet Rupert Brooke, was killed in action in 1915. James's last piece of writing, appropriately, as he would have felt, was an introduction to Brooke's posthumously published *Letters from America* (1916). James also wrote several "war pieces"—on the military hospitals, the American ambulance corps, the Chelsea refugees—which were published as *Within the Rim* (1919) after his death.

Life held two more moments of high significance for Henry James. In July of 1915 he became a British subject by naturalization. A letter to the Prime Minister, the Earl of Oxford and Asquith, expresses his reasons for the change of citizenship:

> I have assiduously and happily spent here all but 40 years, the best years of my life, and I find my wish to testify at this crisis to the force of my attachment and devotion to England, and to the cause for which she is fighting, finally and completely irresistible. . . . I can only testify by laying at her feet my explicit, my material and spiritual allegiance, and throwing into the scale of her fortune my all but imponderable moral weight—"a poor thing but mine own." [41]

Then, in the new-year lists came the announcement that James had been awarded the Order of Merit. It was for him a most gratifying and final recognition.

James had suffered two strokes in quick succession in that December, from which he was unable to recover. He died at the end of February 1916, only a few weeks before his seventy-third birthday. Funeral services were held just a few doors away from his last home, in Chelsea Old Church.

He counted in the circle of his friends and acquaintances many of the important writers and artists of his time in England, France, and America—not a few of them still young men merely of "promise"; with them also he knew many of the important social, political, and financial figures of the day—he was as welcome at the Rothschilds' Mentmore and Waddesden as at the Vanderbilts' Breakers, and at many another great house on both sides of the Atlantic.

[41] *Selected Letters*, p. 228.

He felt that he had never been generally appreciated as a writer, yet before his death he saw one book-length study devoted to his work, Elisabeth Luther Cary's *The Novels of Henry James: A Study;* and in the year of his death two more books devoted to him appeared, Ford Madox Ford's *Henry James: A Critical Study* and Rebecca West's *Henry James*. Like his own Ray Limbert, however, he was deeply appreciated by a select and not so very narrowly restricted band of enlightened admirers. In the years since his death he has come to be fully appreciated as one of the finest novelists of the English-speaking world.

2

FICTION I: THE INTERNATIONAL THEME

HENRY JAMES always regarded *Roderick Hudson* (1876) as his first novel. In 1871 he had published *Watch and Ward* serially in the *Atlantic Monthly,* but it was not published in book form until 1878; and James never included it in any collected edition of his works. There is a peculiar appropriateness in James's giving *Roderick Hudson* the position of primary importance. Just as his initial publication coincided with the death of his early master, Hawthorne, in 1864, so his "first" novel takes up the scene and setting of Hawthorne's last: like *The Marble Faun, Roderick Hudson* deals with American artists in Europe and especially in Rome. This is not to suggest that *Roderick Hudson* simply derives from Hawthorne's novel; James knew at firsthand the American artist colonies in Italy and particularly the group associated with William Wetmore Story, whose biography James would write years later. It is appropriate, furthermore, to begin a review of James's fiction with *Roderick Hudson* because that novel combines two of his major themes—the "international theme" and that of the "dilemma of the artist." Although he would not handle both themes together again in any of his major fiction (and we will discuss the two themes separately), there is special significance in their being combined in this, his first novel—and we shall ultimately return to the question of the significance of that combination.

The story begins in Northampton, Massachusetts, introducing us to Roderick and his fiancée, Mary Garland, and soon to Rowland Mallett. Roderick is an aspiring young sculptor, frustrated both by the stifling cultural poverty of his environment and by the need to devote most of his energy to earning a living. An offer to remove these frustrations from Roderick's life is made by Rowland Mallett, a young man of means and taste and no responsibilities, who sees promise in what little Roderick has been able to create: he offers his patronage and removal to Europe.

The central problem of the novel is thus introduced by Rowland's offer: it raises the question of what is the right line of action for a young American artist to pursue. Although Roderick's statue of the youth drinking (which first roused Rowland's interest) attests clearly enough to his talent, there still remains the question of the sufficiency of the American scene—especially in Northampton—for an artist's needs. Rowland's cousin Cecilia, who seems sophisticated and shrewd, doubts the wisdom of the plan for Roderick's expatriation; the modest young painter Singleton marvels at the ability of Northampton to inspire the creation of the drinking statue—thereby casting further doubt on the proposed move to Europe. The true Northamptonians—the solid and severely practical Mr. Striker, who is Roderick's employer; the timid and ineffectual mother, Mrs. Hudson; and the quiet and plainly pleasant Mary Garland, Roderick's sweetheart—are all opposed to Rowland's plan; their opposition is based on timidity, or understandable possessiveness, or provincialism and mere mercenary practicality. The statue itself—"Thirst"— seems clearly enough, however, to symbolize the yearning and the sense of deprivation of the artist himself. Roderick is eager to go; Rowland urges persuasively. They finally decide to depart for Europe.

Once in the rich and fertile ambience of Rome, Roderick initially flourishes: his huge accomplishment of the "Adam and Eve" is acclaimed, and the rightness of his decision to leave America seems confirmed. Further confirmation is apparently added by the introduction of the beautiful and fascinating Christina Light. As Christina seems to be—and to promise—everything that the simple Mary Garland is not, so Europe seems to Roderick everything that America is not: the one represents satisfaction at every point that the other frustrates him. Both as artist and simply as man, Roderick is delighted by the possibilities dangling before him. Inevitably, however, he begins to show his true New England colors as he feels pangs of guilt over his European enjoyment; he is reminded of his responsibilities to his mother, to Mary, and particularly to Rowland —who is, after all, footing the bill. Rowland in a sense represents Roderick's conscience, reminding him that he must work hard, reminding him of the hope and trust invested in him by the people back home, and reminding him—if only tacitly by his very presence —of the other, more material investment made in him.

Rowland's generosity continues, however, and Roderick is both grateful and resentful. For he wants to succeed artistically, not just commercially. He feels properly indebted to Rowland but cannot force himself to produce works of sculpture merely to answer that debt. And while he is mindful of the hope and trust of those at home, he feels that he cannot deny himself the rich experience, for both man and artist, that Europe offers him. He cannot accept the easy compromise achieved by Gloriani, the popular and successful artist who rejoices in his lionization yet manages to continue producing regularly what people like. The dilemma of Roderick's conflicting desires and affinities plagues him severely and grows particularly acute when his artistic inspiration fails. His tendency then is to plunge himself into the rather frantic pursuit of the rich social experience available to him, a pursuit including that of the fascinating Christina, with whom he believes himself in love. Neither part of the pursuit satisfies him as a man or revives his inspiration as an artist; both tend rather to aggravate his complex feelings of guilt. His problem seems finally to be that while the American atmosphere was too thin to sustain him, the European is richer than he can stand.

The question of Roderick's behavior is to be understood both in terms of art and in terms of social sophistication; ultimately, of course, it is a moral question—but in no narrow sense of the term. Gloriani's rather skeptical attitude toward Roderick's early achievement and his pessimistic prognosis seem to be confirmed: Roderick has aimed too high, has shot his bolt and burned himself out early; he was bound (Gloriani maintained) to falter through careless prodigality of his artistic talents, for he simply would not husband his creative fire, would not school himself in a conserving discipline. The mere presence of Singleton—with his modest and indeed inferior but nonetheless persistent and enduring practice and achievement—seems to substantiate Gloriani's evaluation of Roderick's career. Roderick's indulgence and prodigality in his holidays at the fashionable resorts are the complement of his artistic recklessness. In neither area of his life has Roderick learned—has had neither the occasion nor the opportunity to learn—to manage himself prudently. He has failed, fundamentally, to learn those manners that are essential to make life possible in civilized society. He remains, too often, an eccentric, selfishly and self-indulgently boorish and mannerless—as an artist, finally, as much as a man. The clear waste, the failure of his pursuits outside the studio to function successfully as recreation or even as restorative diversion, reflects Roderick's moral weakness. Surely he would be better off to attend more zealously to the counsel of his friend Rowland, who understands very well the words of Wordsworth's "stern daughter of the voice of God," named Duty, and understands the value of work—unattractive as that often seems to be. Surely he would: but our sympathy remains with him, nevertheless, and we can hardly bring ourselves to condone the dutiful capitulation.

Christina Light is the vexing complication in Roderick's life; she is obviously the kind of lovely creature who would upset any impressionable man, especially a thirsty one from Northampton, Massachusetts, especially if he were also an artist. She inspires both the artist and the man in Roderick. She is beauty's very self, of course, and any artist would rightly desire her; the trouble comes when the man himself desires her—desires to possess her for herself alone. It is thus that Christina assumes the aspect and role of Faust's Marguerite, and Roderick's headlong pursuit of her—for her personal self—proves to be his undoing: it is his abdication as an artist. (That pursuit may also represent the frantic and instantaneous explosion of all his artistic energy—against which Gloriani had warned; the two are not contradictory, for both suggest insufficient control, either of man or of artist.)

The Mephistophelian figure who employs Christina as Marguerite is her mother, Mrs. Light—a Europeanized American (a figure with which we shall become increasingly familiar). On the literal level, the wretched use to which Christina is put makes her as lethal a poisonous dose as Rappaccini's daughter in Hawthorne's tale. She is not herself bad; she is maleficent but not malevolent—and maleficent as a result of her mother's evil manipulations. Figuratively, the distinction is not so easy to make: in any case she is a bad goal to seek. She is, whether she will or not, the undoing of Roderick. On the other hand, that undoing points up the personal and moral weakness of Roderick, his malleability.

Poor Roderick's dilemma is further complicated by the arrival of his mother and Mary Garland, and the contrast between Christina and Mary is sharply underlined. Mary is still the faultless, dutiful, pretty, housewifely, loyal New England girl; she is to Christina what Thackeray's Amelia is to Becky Sharp. Yet she is more than that, for if she is innocent and ignorant of the ways of the great world, she is sensitive and intelligent and will learn. Miss Garland blossoms in the European soil and will return to America—even without Roderick—richer and wiser than she left it. Of course Rowland is in love with her! But how can Roderick possibly return to her? How can he see what she has become when his eye is dazzled by the brilliant Christina Light? Roderick cannot be satisfied with what he left behind; he cannot grasp the wonderful things he has discovered in Europe—for they are corrupt and corrupting, poisoned by the cupidity, the inhuman manipulation and coercion of which Christina is the victim. There is no way out for Roderick; his desperate flight ends in suicide.

The novel presents us with a nice balance of the conflicting values that plague Roderick and fix him in frustrating inability to choose. The thinness and insufficiency of the life he left behind is balanced by its unmistakable goodness, simplicity, and homely virtue. The rich and stimulating variety of the new life he finds in Europe is balanced by its corruption, its carelessness of human integrity, and its mercenary view of the individual. The unhappy career of Roderick Hudson expresses a cautionary word about the dangers that lie in wait in the great wide world to ensnare the unprepared and the unwary; but it also faces—with a touch of reluctance—the necessity of leaving the nest and bravely venturing into that world, as a condition of maturity. And in those very terms it also speaks to the beginning artist—especially the American artist, like Henry James himself—who must sally forth into the world where rich experience awaits, into the great old world of Europe, in fact, as a risk to be run for the sake of his artistic development. Life is an adventure that must be met, fraught though it be with dreadful difficulties.

Roderick Hudson has significance beyond the terms of its story; its surface is faithfully realistic, based on James's firsthand experience. Nevertheless, he has managed to use the surface realism so as to suggest broader implications, giving his novel almost a metaphorical quality. James was fortunate in the material that lay at hand, or at least in what he saw in that material. One of his earliest short stories to develop the international theme casts some useful light on the question of James's raw material and the possibilities he saw in it. "A Passionate Pilgrim" (1871), which gave its title to James's first volume of short stories in 1875, has an almost mythical quality as it relates the adventure of an American, Clement Searle, who visits the English home of distant cousins and learns to feel that he really belongs there. Clement, who bears the name of a great-uncle who perished on board ship as a young man bound for America, says in a kind of reverie: "His spirit came ashore and wandered forlorn till it got lodgement again in my poor body. In my poor body it has lived, homesick, these forty years." [1] At the outset of the story the narrator makes an observation that lends brilliant illumination not only to this short story but, as I say, to all of James's international fiction.

The latent preparedness of the American mind for even the most delectable features of English life is a fact which I never fairly probed to its depths. The roots of it are so deeply buried in the virgin soil of our primary culture, that, without some great upheaval of experience, it would be hard to say exactly when and where and how it begins. It makes an American's enjoyment of England an emotion more fatal and sacred than his enjoyment, say, of Italy or Spain. [2]

The "fact" which this fictional narrator relates is one that James himself had had ample opportunity to observe in his own life and milieu on both sides of the Atlantic. It provided him with the terms of his international metaphor.

It appears again in *The American,* published a year after *Roderick Hudson. The American* is an inferior novel but a popular one probably because in a manner it "solves" its problem and clearly enough points its moral. It is the story of a wealthy American who comes to Europe to buy a generous slice of culture: he has the money and wants not only the biggest pictures (or copies of them) but the best wife that money can buy. Of course Europe, always gracefully accommodating, disposes itself to comply with his wishes. Christopher Newman, our hero, finds himself enamored of Claire de Cintré, widowed daughter of the Bellegarde family in Paris. Although the Bellegardes are impressed by his credentials—that is, the length of his purse—they are dismayed by his manners, or his lack of them, and at last find him unsuitable as a prospective son-in-law. Claire is forbidden him, even though she is favorably disposed toward him, and even though the younger brother, Valentin, also befriends him. Finally Claire is placed in maximum security by being "persuaded" to enter a convent and take the veil. Christopher is then put in possession of secret information about the skeleton in the Bellegarde closet, which promises to be the lever by means of which he can pry Claire loose from the family. He confronts the mother and

---

[1] *The Complete Tales of Henry James,* ed. Leon Edel (Philadelphia and New York: J. B. Lippincott Company, 1962), II, 256.
[2] *Tales,* II, 227.

older brother, Urbain, with his weapon; yet at the last moment he decides that it would be a dastardly trick to use the weapon, would lower him to their level by involving him in their foul game. He destroys the information and returns to America a somewhat sadder but a wiser and nobler man than he left it.

It is, apparently, a story of the triumph of American good-heartedness over European corruption; yet before Christopher is allowed his moral triumph, he is exposed to a great deal of sharply satirical treatment. If the fine manners of the representative Europeans do seem to hide a multitude of sins, Claire and Valentin are surely possessed of the same basic goodness that animates Christopher. Here the typical international theme receives a balanced and clear-cut exposition: the good and the bad of both the American and the European are distinctly and carefully set forth. Christopher is basically good-hearted and well intentioned, yet his woeful naïveté is so extreme as actually to constitute a serious fault—especially when seen against the background of European cultured civilization. Newman is the great Western barbarian, the hick, a boor and a bear: he is unfinished man. The European Bellegardes are awfully (in the most literal sense) well mannered, are of course as much at ease in society's drawing room as Newman is awkward. They are girded by tradition and guided by convention, and beneath their elegant façade there seems to beat no heart at all. Valentin is the striking exception, an expressive counterpart to Christopher Newman. Valentin's fundamental goodness is still perfectly visible even though it is threatened constantly by the dictates of manners and convention. His death, indeed, is an eloquent comment on the situation: the convention of the duel and the misguided chivalric tradition combine to kill young Valentin.

James drew upon his familiarity with romance literature to add emphasis and give shape to the novel—for example, the old romance of Valentin and Orson, twins separated at birth and raised separately, Valentin at court and Orson in the woods by a bear, only to meet later and prove invincible when reunited. Valentin is obviously Valentin, and Christopher is often enough likened to a bear and at least once specifically to Orson, to make this indebtedness sufficiently apparent. More obviously, however, *The American* derives from Hawthornesque romance and, beyond that, from European (especially English) romance fiction—including the Gothic. The cloak-and-dagger atmosphere, thickened by the dark family secret and its awful revelation by the old family retainer, Mrs. Bread, puts this early novel of James's directly in the romance tradition. But something also comes from Dickens—not least the heavily suggestive nomenclature. A good deal of the novel's meaning, in fact, is underlined by the names of persons and places. The hero's name surely strikes the reader like a Mack Sennett custard pie—Christopher Newman. The sternly protective Bellegardes are significantly named Urbain, Claire, Valentin; and the daughter Claire, who most feels the force of the encircling protection of the family is appropriately named Cintré (the word has the suggestion of "confined," connected as it is with *ceinture,* belt or girdle, and the related *enceinte,* confined or pregnant). There is even a naughty suggestiveness in Nioche, the surname of Noémie, the young lady of various talents (all apparently for hire) who provides Christopher with his introduction to the largess of the Louvre. It is fitting, too, that the convent in which the reluctant Claire is incarcerated should be located in the Rue d'Enfer—Hell Street!—and that she should take the name of Sister Veronica, as a reminder, perhaps, of her close association, however brief, with Christopher.

The play with names is typically enough Jamesian, though a bit more unrestrained than usual here. He would always rely on the suggestiveness and significance of names (his Notebooks are full of lists culled from newspapers). Some of them blossom wonderfully in his stories—not simply the euphonious Ruck, Beck, Vetch, and Stant, but the angelic Ralph (Touchett), Gabriel (Nash), and Gabrielle (de Bergerac); the apostolic Sir Luke of Harley Street and Lord Mark of Venice; and the quaintly and queerly appropriate Birdseye, Ulick, Fleda, and the striking Mallett (the force behind Roderick Hudson's sculptor's chisel). But in *The American* the nomenclature amounts almost to a set of labels and contributes much to the rather allegorical aspect of the novel. That feature, combined with the heavy-handed Gothicism of its romantic denouement, accounts largely for the dissatisfaction one feels with *The American*; so that even the delightful humor—and it is a humorous book—does not sufficiently save it for us.

It is, nevertheless, an instructive novel for the student of James. The way in which James has developed the international material and apportioned his value system here sets up a pattern to which his subsequent fiction remains strikingly constant. There is one important exception to that. In *The American* the representatives of the old traditional society and the potential evil therein are all Europeans; in virtually all his other stories on the international theme the American innocent is opposed to, not principally Europeans but, Europeanized Americans, like Mrs. Light in *Roderick Hudson.* The importance of that exception is that it enables us to see that James is typically interested only secondarily or superficially in the contrast of national cultures and societies in themselves, that his fundamental interest is with the effect of those contrasting cultures on the American character as a means of expressing his ultimate concern with the question of cultural maturity and its relation to moral maturity. In the typical international stories the American protagonist is at bottom simply Man confronting the rich and complex and complicated possibilities of life and its attendant pitfalls and threats; he is only secondarily an American.

But even in saying so, one is aware of the inadequacy of the terms: for the Americanism of the protagonist does matter very much. The point is, as was suggested in making reference to "A Passionate Pilgrim," that James found in the actual situation of real Americans confronted by the European scene material that was in its very nature admirably suited to express his ideas about life and the general human condition as he understood it. He had only to give a fairly faithful reproduction of life as it appeared to him at that time in order to find a realistic, rich, and satisfying metaphoric medium of expression for his truths about mankind.

The trouble with *The American,* apparently, is that James did not recognize those possibilities or was unable to realize them fully. A helpful suggestion is offered by Oscar Cargill in *The Novels of Henry James*:[3] James was put off by the rough treatment of Americans in Dumas's play *L'Etrangère,* of which he wrote an irritated review for the New York *Tribune* when he was partway through the novel; he turned *The American* to the business of justifying his compatriots. For if on the one hand the novel is too obviously metaphoric, threatening indeed to stiffen into allegory; on the other it is too vigorously chauvinistic. As Constance Rourke has admirably said,[4] Christopher Newman derives from a prominent figure in American folklore—the simple good man, the diamond in the rough. Another version of him appeared in the figure of Lincoln—at least the Lincoln of our myths—and such motion picture heroes as Gary Cooper and John Wayne: he has no fancy manners but a tough hide and a heart of gold. He is, as previously mentioned, the great Western barbarian,

---

[3] (New York: Macmillan, 1961), pp. 43ff.
[4] *American Humor: A Study of the National Character* (New York: Harcourt, Brace & World, 1931), pp. 235–265.

but also the noble savage dear to Rousseau's and our heart. To be sure, James has some fun at Newman's expense; he even awakens our regret at Newman's approach to art and matrimony—an approach appropriate to the floor of the Bourse. Yet we are never permitted to forget his good-heartedness, to overlook the evil that lies behind the lovely manners of the Bellegardes and their coterie, to miss the point that the few good characters on the European scene are recognizable by their appreciation of Newman's essential goodness. We are almost tempted to say that Claire de Cintré takes the name Veronica less in honor of the saint than out of romantic nostalgia for Christopher. *The American* seems to be social comment masquerading in allegorical fiction, or perhaps a melodrama of manners. It fails, really, to dilate the imagination, and tends instead to dictate the extended application of its significance rather than imply or suggest it—as all art must do if it is to succeed.

Between the publication of *The American* and James's first masterpiece, *The Portrait of a Lady* (1880–1881), he published a number of short pieces of fiction that develop the international theme in interesting ways—refining his conceptions and sharpening the focus of his ideas. His problem was to clarify the terms of the polarity he had set up—Europe vis-à-vis America—by sorting out for examination the characteristics of the two poles, between which the tension of his fictional dramas is suspended, to clarify and particularly to evaluate them.

He considered and reconsidered the comparative *innocence* of his American hero or heroine—a state created by the youth of the country, and by its lack of traditions and (as James increasingly felt) of a richly cultural civilization, a state perpetuated and complicated by America's religious or at least its *moral* tone. He questioned acutely the sufficiency for effective civilized life of the good-hearted but ingenuous and naïve American. At the same time he weighed the merits and weaknesses of representatives of that traditional, conventional, and strictly mannered society into the midst of which the inexperienced hero is set to perform and against which his peculiar American qualities are tested.

In the midst of this cluster of short stories, James published an unsigned article in *The Nation*, "Americans Abroad," [5] in which he addressed specifically and discursively the very matter he was dealing with in his international fiction: "the question of Americans

---

[5] XXVII (October 3, 1878), 208–209.

appearing 'to advantage' or otherwise in Europe." The article is an
attempt at a balanced treatment of the question; it explains why
Europeans have difficulty understanding the American abroad and
appreciating the merits of the democratic country he has left, sometimes only to visit but increasingly to settle for an extended period
in Europe: "it is not surprising that [the Europeans] should be
found doubting whether the country the American has left is as
agreeable, as comfortable, as civilized, as desirable a one as [their]
own. . . . the fact remains that in pursuit of some *agrément* or
other he has forsaken his native land. . . ." It also explains why,
on the other hand, the American fails to make himself and his country understood by the Europeans. In spite of the attempt, however,
it is easy to see where James's sympathies lie: he cannot help but
regret that his compatriots do not make a better showing abroad.

> The great innocence of the usual American tourist is perhaps his most
> general quality. He takes all sorts of forms, some of them agreeable
> and some the reverse, and it is probably not unfair to say that by
> sophisticated Europeans it is harshly interpreted. . . . they set it
> down once for all as vulgar. . . . Their merits, whatever they are,
> are not of a sort that strike the eye—still less the ear. They are
> ill-made, ill-mannered, ill-dressed.

The essence of those last two sentences is, in one way or another,
at the heart of all of James's stories on the international theme.

"Four Meetings" (1877) tells of the pathetic little schoolmistress,
Caroline Spencer, who is cheated of her experience of Europe—for
which she has carefully saved her pennies for years—by the trickery
of her nasty art-student cousin. Miss Spencer is a babe in the woods;
and once out of the protective safety of her significantly named home
town of Grimwinter, she is singularly incapable of coping with the
world. She is innocent, naïve, of severely limited experience, and
romantically attracted to Europe—she has read her Byron. Our first
glimpse of her in the story strikes the essential note of her character
—childlikeness:

> Miss Caroline Spencer was not exactly a beauty, but she was a
> charming little figure. She must have been close upon thirty, but she
> was made almost like a little girl, and she had the complexion of a
> child.[6]

---

[6] *Tales,* IV, 88; subsequent references are in the text.

Another touch is given her characterization by the narrator's calling her "a thin-stemmed, mild-hued flower of Puritanism." (IV, 95) The extent and significance of her range of experience is given, in an exchange with the narrator, not simply by the facts of her account but especially in the tone:

> . . . I asked her if she had always lived at Grimwinter.
> "Oh, no sir," said Miss Spencer. "I have spent twenty-three months in Boston." (IV, 92)

A summing up of Caroline Spencer—and of many other Jamesian heroines—is given in the closing lines of the first section of the story:

> "I understand your case," I rejoined. "You have the native American passion—the passion for the picturesque. With us, I think, it is primordial—antecedent to experience. Experience comes and only shows us something we have dreamt of." (IV, 92)

Miss Spencer is a lamb ripe for the sacrifice (a figure James would add in his revision of the story for inclusion in the New York Edition of his works); and when her wretched cousin tells her, in Le Havre, his fanciful story of his wife—a Countess (he claims) whose family has disapproved of their marriage—Caroline finds it only too romantic and touching and turns over to him all her savings, much to the exasperated chagrin of the narrator.

Years later the narrator finds Caroline at her home in Grimwinter (James would soften the touch of that bald name in his revision by substituting the faintly ironic North Verona). She has never been able to return to Europe, but now has a bit of Europe with her in America: her cousin's "Countess" is living with and *off* her. The narrator's description of the Countess makes it clear that his experienced eye detects an impostor:

> Whither was it the sight of her seemed to transport me? To some dusky landing before a shabby Parisian *quatrième*—to an open door revealing a greasy ante-chamber, and to Madame leaning over the banisters while she holds a faded dressing-gown together and bawls down to the portress to bring up her coffee. (IV, 111)

He leaves the pathetic Caroline, adding no comment to her that might truly enlighten her to the state of her victimization, and allowing himself only the ironic reflection that "Miss Spencer had been right in her presentiment that she should still see something of that dear old Europe." (IV, 118)

The emotional point of the story is sharply made: pathetic as poor Caroline is, she has virtually invited her catastrophe; her miserably thin and poor training for the reality of life has prepared her only to accept this catastrophe—as we clearly understand it. Much of the pathos, indeed, derives from her not really recognizing it as a catastrophe, from her meekly persisting in a faded romantic dream— persisting in ignorance. Yet her catastrophe needs its villain; her unscrupulous and scheming cousin fills that role. He is of course American, an American partly "Europeanized"—his experience abroad has given him the thinnest veneer of artistic culture (through which the narrator and we can see with ease). But it is important to notice that James has shifted the role of villain from a European (as it was in *The American*) to an American character. Certainly the phony Countess is distinctly unpleasant and quite hateful in her treatment of Caroline; but she is the cousin's responsibility and his legacy to the unfortunate Caroline. The story focuses principally, however, on Caroline Spencer's lack of preparation for life, on her almost willing acceptance of victimization, and only secondarily on those whose victim she becomes. Its theme is the insufficiency of American civilization.

The famous "Daisy Miller" (1878) presents an extreme case of aggressive American naïveté, beside which the gentle willingness of Caroline to be devoured pales pathetically. Daisy Miller is a flirt, yet really not a bad sort at all. She is almost tragically uninformed and quite without the benefit of mature guidance—her wretched mother is a distinct liability!—and she has the fiercely assertive self-confidence that ignorance and parental indulgence combine to foster. She behaves in Europe as she has behaved at home; and when her would-be friends Winterbourne and Mrs. Walker attempt to counsel her against her "free" behavior—which will be grossly misunderstood—Daisy merely becomes all the more contrary and more determined than ever to do exactly what she wants. She knows that she means no harm and is amazed that anyone should think she does. The trouble is, of course, that Daisy Miller does not really know what the "harm" in question might be. To tell her that she is behaving like a streetwalker would provoke her to reply simply that she likes walking the streets, and where's the harm in that? The attention given her by Giovanelli, the opportunistic little Italian; the lack of understanding shown her (as she thinks) by Mrs. Walker and the finally bewildered Winterbourne; and the refusal of the rest of the American community at last to have anything to do with her drive Daisy more deliberately than ever on her downward path. She just will not learn, will not be told, will not *see;* and she plunges pigheadedly on to her doom, poor little fool!

At the end of the story Winterbourne learns from Giovanelli, at her graveside, that to the end she was innocent. Winterbourne is of course affected by her death, and finds "it was on his conscience that he had done her injustice." [7] His explanation of that—"I was booked to make a mistake. I've lived too long in foreign parts." (XVIII, 93)—has been seized on by scores of readers who fail to see Daisy's culpability and who then put full blame for her catastrophe on Winterbourne's shoulders. If it seems to us that he is another of those Europeanized Americans who we said are typically responsible for the evil that strikes the innocent American hero or heroine, we have failed to take into account his scruples and his quite unselfish interest in Daisy's welfare—her not appearing worse than she is—and we have forgotten that he is the last and the most reluctant to give up on her. He is by all odds the most sympathetic to Daisy and wants to think the best of her: "it was painful [to him] to see so much that was pretty and undefended and natural sink so low in human estimation." (XVIII, 78) But he is finally so puzzled by her behavior—and after the most friendly and unselfish advice—that he is almost ready to agree in her general condemnation. He wonders "how far her extravagance was generic and national and how far it was crudely personal." (XVIII, 81) After all, the supposition that she has regrettably become "engaged" to Giovanelli has acted as an impediment to his further action. The point of the story is surely that Winterbourne cannot, with the best intentions and the greatest goodwill possible, be sure that he is not being *taken in* by the little flirt: he wants to think well of her, but her actions and the opinion of all the others in his circle prevent his doing so. We ought, too, to look again at the representation of her death: it has an almost symbolic value. She has been warned against visiting the Colosseum by moonlight; we know that only Giovanelli would take her. Refusing to accept the friendly advice to do as must be done in Rome, Daisy chooses to go directly into

[7] *The Novels and Tales of Henry James* (New York: Charles Scribner's Sons, 1962–1965), XVIII, 93; subsequent references are in the text.

the jaws of death that lie in wait for those who will not learn prudence.

James has shifted his emphasis in this story to indicate the importance of manners to the smooth functioning of social intercourse in civilized society: they are the expressive means by which one may successfully communicate in a civilized way and so be known for what one is. He condemns the American failure to adopt expressive manners intelligently, and points out the folly of believing that a good heart is readily visible to all—despite the evidence of one's actions.

Perhaps we can understand poor foolish Daisy even better after reading *The Europeans* (1878). If "Daisy Miller" raised with particular urgency the question of what manners are for, *The Europeans* examines the question of what is the happiest function of manners —and finds its answer in the character of its hero. The international situation is somewhat reversed in this story, for here the Europeans visit America: Eugenia, Baroness Münster of Silberstadt, and her younger brother Felix, a decidedly minor but highly good-natured artist, descend upon the Wentworth household in the country just outside Boston. But these Europeans and Americans are truly cousins, for the Europeans are in this case of American parentage; and the concerns to which this novella addresses itself, at least through all the rich thickness of its deep realistic surface, are peculiarly American. The story tests the sufficiency of American standards—esthetic, social, and, most important, moral—by introducing the truly Europeanized sister and brother, *nés* Young, to our native milieu. This change of venue from the European stage to the American permits James to throw a fuller and more broadly searching light on the American scene. It also serves to emphasize James's intention of dealing more particularly with American problems of life —or rather with the human condition in more strictly American terms.

The portrait of the Wentworth family and their friends the Actons is fundamentally sympathetic, yet it does highlight the stiffness, dryness, and angularity of the American and especially the New England way of life. The Baroness finds the place on the whole depressingly provincial. Felix finds it a comical country but yet delightful; his foreign eye catches its essential pristine goodness. He describes for his sister the Wentworths' setting as "intensely rural, tremendously natural; and all overhung with this strange white light, this faraway blue sky."[8] And even Eugenia in her best moments can concur: she finds the Wentworth household "pervaded by a sort of dove-coloured freshness. . . . It was all very good, very innocent and safe, and out of it something good must come." (p. 71) We are soon made to feel with Felix that the chief "something good" is Gertrude Wentworth. Yet with all his sympathetic appreciation of the place and its way of life, Felix puts his finger squarely on its weakness. He accepts the "plain, homely way of life" but acutely regrets that it has "nothing for show, and very little for—what shall I call it—for the senses." (p. 57) (Felix is in fact echoing the sentiments of James's father, who felt that in Europe his children would get a much better sensual education than they could in America.) He explains to his sister that the Wentworths are not gay, are sober, even severe: "they take things hard." (p. 58) And he manages to sum up the essence of their being in his pithy vignette of the head of the household: "My uncle, Mr. Wentworth, is a tremendously high-toned old fellow; he looks as if he were undergoing martyrdom, not by fire, but by freezing." (p. 58)

The cadence to which the Wentworths strictly march is called by that stern daughter of the voice of God, Duty. They cannot permit themselves to enjoy, to be pleased; their highest satisfaction comes in their recognition of a duty to be performed. Even the visit of their European cousins, a great event in their life, they regard as "an extension of duty, of the exercise of the more recondite virtues; but neither Mr. Wentworth, nor Charlotte, nor Mr. Brand . . . frankly adverted to it as an extension of enjoyment." (p. 66) For life, according to the New England conscience, is for discipline, not pleasure.

The daughter Gertrude, unlike her sister Charlotte, is uneasy under this rigorous discipline; and we are quite able to understand Felix's attraction to her. In this blossoming relationship the principal dramatic interest of the story is focused. Felix is reticent, for he believes that Gertrude already has an "understanding" with Mr. Brand, who thinks so too! But Gertrude does her best to discourage Brand; and when Felix at last feels that the way is open to him he undertakes benevolently to "awaken" Gertrude to the possibilities of true enjoyment and to win her away—again benevolently—from the stifling influence of the New England manner. The climax of the drama

[8] *The American Novels and Stories of Henry James*, ed. F. O. Matthiessen (New York: Alfred A. Knopf, 1947), p. 57; subsequent references are in the text.

perhaps occurs in the catechetical dialogue between him and Gertrude on the subject of life's purpose. She has admitted that "We are not fond of amusement." (p. 82)

". . . But you take a painful view of life, as one might say."
"One ought to think it bright and charming and delightful, eh?" asked Gertrude.
"I should say so—if one can. It all depends upon that," Felix added.
. . . "To 'enjoy' " she began at last, "to take life—not painfully, must one do something wrong?"

"I don't think it's what one does or doesn't do that promotes enjoyment," her companion answered. "It is the general way of looking at life."
"They look at it as a discipline—that is what they do here. I have often been told that."
"Well, that's very good. But there is another way," added Felix, smiling: "to look at it as an opportunity." (p. 83)

As a result of this discussion, containing the essence of James's pervading attitude to life, Gertrude is awakened—she comes alive to the basic urgings of her own best nature. Finally she asserts herself and her needs to her family and accepts Felix. The family has remained mildly puzzled by Felix and therefore is just a little suspicious of this figure whom it cannot quite understand. His ways—his manners—are strange to it. Yet in her urgent demand to be free to accept Felix, Gertrude attacks the manners of her New England ambience and makes her claim for naturalness. The family reminds her that she has always had a "difficult temperament"; "It might have been easy, if you had allowed it," she replies. "You wouldn't let me be natural." (p. 153)

Again, the rigorous grip of manners is presented as the evil of the piece. But in the relationship of Felix and Gertrude the American, not the European, convention of behavior is the culprit. Felix's European manners, indeed, come in for direct praise: "Felix had at all times the brilliant assurance of manner which was simply the vehicle of his good spirits and his good will." (p. 134) The distinction is clear: that manner of behavior that is truly expressive of an individual's being and therefore permits honest communication and understanding among people is good; that manner that is *representational* rather than truly expressive—which *stands for* qualities, so to speak, symbolically—is bad, deceptive, dangerous, and destructive. The former is comparable to art, the latter to artifice.

The other side of the same coin is shown in the role of the Baroness, especially in her relations with Robert Acton. She is a considerable puzzle to the Wentworths, of course: she is "too polite," (p. 67) and she clearly tells fibs. If her manners are a rather cloying sugar-coating to her person, they do not suffer unduly by comparison with the naked mannerlessness of, say, young Clifford. Yet Clifford's insufficient social nudity is at least honest; Eugenia's manners, finally, are deceptive and dishonest. The sophisticated Robert Acton finds them semiopaque and almost makes out the honest essence of Eugenia. It is a significant touch that during their sojourn together at blessed Newport they are closest and there almost reach an understanding. Finally, however, Robert finds that Eugenia is too far committed to manners alone, has too little of her real self left to give him.

Yet on the whole the story ends happily: it almost overwhelms us, in fact, with marriages and happiness ever after. This was quite intentional on James's part, as he was annoyed with critical objection to his pessimistic endings; he was determined to offer ample compensation! Most significant of all is the meaning of the union of Felix and Gertrude, a union that almost realizes James's ideal reconciliation of American and European qualities—"manners" happily wedded to "morals": Felix has the manners of a civilized gentleman and the sufficient good-heartedness and clear vision to see the virtue beneath the rather ungainly moralistic rigor of the New England conscience; Gertrude's good-heartedness and willing naturalness is freed by unselfish love from the somewhat wrongheaded, restricting grip of New England moralism, and she is awakened to the esthetic or "sensual" opportunities of life. Nothing good has been lost, and only good has been gained.

Another balanced treatment of the international theme, one which has also marked similarities to "Four Meetings," however, is "An International Episode" (1878–1879). It offers a direct, bipartisan confrontation of Americans and Europeans, both in America and in Europe. It has all the appearance of a comedy of manners: its dramatic ado derives from the clash of European manners and conventions with American behavior. James begins his double-edged satire with the arrival in New York of Percy Beaumont and Lord Lambeth: the flatness and the uncouth edge of American life in its virtually traditionless novelty are exposed through the supercilious view of Beaumont and Lambeth. Yet they are themselves satirized—

their stuffiness and stiffness and inflated condescension—by their
very view of things in New York.

Of quite other sense and sound from those of any typical English
street was the endless rude channel, rich in incongruities, through
which our two travellers advanced—looking out on either side at the
rough animation of the sidewalks, at the high-coloured heterogeneous
architecture, at the huge white marble facades that, bedizened with
gilded lettering, seemed to glare in the strong crude light, at the multi-
farious awnings, banners and streamers, at the extraordinary numbers
of omnibuses, horse-cars and other democratic vehicles, at the vendors
of cooling fluids, the white trousers and big straw hats of the police-
men, the tripping gait of the modish young persons on the pavement,
the general brightness, newness, juvenility, both of people and things.
The young men had exchanged few observations, but in crossing Union
Square . . . one of them remarked to the other: "Awfully rum place."

They are rescued from the hellish heat of New York and conveyed
to the heavenly coolness (the comparison is James's) of Newport
on the invitation of the Westgate family; and Beaumont and Lambeth are there paired off with Mrs. Westgate and Bessie Alden. The
principal *dramatis personae* are on stage together, and the particular
agon begins.

The flat loquaciousness of Mrs. Westgate's boastful apologia for
the American way—in which she denies apology and "blowing"!—
contrasts with the laconic piquancy of Beaumont's utterances. But
the focus quickly fixes on Lambeth and Bessie Alden. Bessie is a
younger and more intelligent Caroline Spencer. She is innocent, artless, direct. Like Caroline she is possessed of "the native American
passion" for the picturesque (the revised version calls it, less gently,
"the great American disease"): Bessie "was very fond of the poets
and historians, of the picturesque, of the past, of associations, of
relics and reverberations of greatness." [9] Having read a good deal
about Europe and especially about England, Bessie is romantically
interested in the handsome representative of that wonderful realm.
Lord Lambeth returns the interest: his simple good-heartedness responds to the fresh young American in spite of the constant cautionary admonitions of Percy Beaumont, who is suspicious of all young
women who show an interest in Lambeth.

While the relationship flourishes pleasantly and harmlessly in the

---

[9] *Novels and Tales*, XIV, 331; subsequent references are in the text.

almost Edenic Newport, it is necessarily altered in the heavier atmosphere of the Old World. Mrs. Westgate, acceptable at home, becomes brittle, suspicious, and feline (her name is Kitty) in England. The conventional, tradition-bound Old World prevents Lambeth and Bessie from "being themselves," from enjoying the easy and natural association they had previously known. Mrs. Westgate sophisticatedly explains that "Newport isn't London. At Newport he could do as he liked, but here it's another affair." (XIV, 341) Bessie is of course suspected by Lambeth's family of trying to "catch" him—his title and estates and position. And that suspicion is in turn early suspected by Mrs. Westgate, who determines to try her hand at one-upmanship and frighten the family by pricking it where it is most sensitive. Lambeth in his simplicity is largely unaware of the maneuvering. Bessie, also unaware but sensitive to differences, resembles a little the porcocephalic Daisy Miller in her somewhat rigid insistence on her right to act as naturally here as she had at home.

The crisis is provoked when Lambeth invites his American friends to Branches Castle (his home), and his mother and sisters to come and meet his friends. The substantial Duchess, Lambeth's mamma, makes a preliminary visit to Bessie. The crucial exchange between the suspicious Duchess and the guileless Bessie is given most effective dramatic treatment:

> "I quite yearn to see it—to see the Castle," Bessie went on to the larger lady. "I've never seen one—in England at least; and you know we've none in America."
>
> "Ah you're fond of Castles?"—her Grace quite took it up.
>
> "Of the idea of them—which is all I know—immensely." And the girl's pale light deepened for the assurance. "It has been the dream of my life to live in one."
>
> The Duchess looked at her as if hardly knowing how to take such words, which, from the ducal point of view, had either to be very artless or very aggressive. (XIV, 386)

The brief subsequent conversation between Mrs. Westgate and Bessie opens the latter's eyes to what the Duchess had been *up to*—although not quite to what Mrs. Westgate had been up to. The story ends with a sadder and wiser Bessie canceling her plans to visit Branches and turning young Lambeth away. The chief victim of the lack of understanding and rapport is perhaps Lord Lambeth. It might seem that he, like Valentin of *The American,* has been victimized by the conventions and customs of his society. The difficulty is that both he and Bessie suffer in the highly mannered world of Europe, where naturalness cannot function. Natural behavior fails where only mannered deportment is understood: for mannered deportment is not expressive but representational.

Bessie has been affected by her experience—though the depth of her feeling for Lambeth is left unclear—and she earns our sympathy. If she has suffered from being misunderstood through her artless honesty, the particular villain of the piece is not of the European world: it is Mrs. Westgate. The aptly named Kitty has interfered in human affairs to manipulate them for her own satisfaction. If left alone the Duchess just might have discovered that Bessie was "very artless"; but Kitty Westgate must assert her equality (at least) by attempting to beat the Duchess at what she takes to be her own game. The Duchess with Bessie might well have been seeking the truth; Kitty was seeking sport.

Mrs. Westgate is not quite the Europeanized American who will dominate the villain's role in much of James's subsequent international fiction, but she has been much influenced by her European experience and dons the European style (as she believes) like a thin cloak to deal with the Europeans on their terms. As it turns out, in so doing she is false to her best self and also, it becomes increasingly clear in the light of James's later stories, false to the best European manners.

THE PORTRAIT OF A LADY

The Portrait of a Lady (1880–1881) is the first full-blown example of James's ability to realize the metaphoric possibilities of his realistic subject, the social comedy of manners. Here the realistic elements of geographic setting, architectural structures, social institutions, and physical posture of characters, aided by apparently simple and adequate figurative language, are made to give resonance and depth of significance to the story. Through repetition and careful placing of emphasis, those elements come to mean much more than they simply *say*.

James had begun work on the *Portrait* by the middle seventies, when he was busy writing the short stories we have just been considering; and from the beginning he knew it would be something special, something other than those stories on a similar theme that he still regarded as journeyman work. He wrote to his mother to say that these others would be to the *Portrait* as water unto wine.[10] It dealt with a subject that had always fascinated him, of course; but as he conceived it now, he recognized it as something very close to his heart. As the novel began its serial publication in *Macmillan's Magazine* and the *Atlantic Monthly,* his friend Grace Norton wrote to say that she recognized in Isabel Archer a marked indebtedness to Minny Temple. In his reply James politely agreed that there was something of Minny there; he did not point out that the principal indebtedness to his cousin was to be found in a male character— Ralph Touchett! That, as we shall see, is much more nearly the truth.

Like Minny, however, Isabel Archer is a fresh young American with a great desire for life, and blessed with the quality of "moral spontaneity," which James cherished in American girls like Minny Temple and Clover Hooper (who would become Mrs. Henry Adams).[11] She is typically innocent, naïve, and ignorant; and she is introduced early to the Old World that is Europe—a world of deep experience, long traditions, firm conventions, and established institutions. In her cheerful ignorance she believes she is independent and earnestly wishes to remain so—to be free to see life. In this belief she refuses the proposals of marriage to her by Lord Warburton and her persistent American suitor, Caspar Goodwood: she wants to remain free and uncommitted and above all independent of the solicitous protection of a husband. Unlike Daisy Miller, Isabel is aware of her own inexperience and ignorance and wishes to repair that flaw in her life that would leave her an incomplete woman. This quality of brave eagerness to see life and affront her destiny strongly attracts the benevolent interest of her cousin Ralph Touchett. Convinced that Isabel deserves every chance to realize her ambition, Ralph persuades his ailing father to alter his will so as to transfer from Ralph to Isabel a bequest of £70.000 (equivalent to something like half a million dollars today)—requiring only that his role in the arrangement remain secret. Yet we understand Ralph's mild apprehensiveness at the risk involved in bestowing that much freedom on Isabel, whose innocence and good-hearted ignorance make her particularly vulnerable to the evil snares of a knowing Old World ("she had seen very little of the evil of the world.").[12] Even Isabel herself, for all her wish to be free to see life, recognizes what her inheritance means. She explains her fears to Ralph—in terms we shall have oc-

---

[10] See *Selected Letters,* p. 52.
[11] *Letters,* I, 26.
[12] *Novels and Tales,* III, 69; subsequent references are in the text.

casion to recall vividly: "A large fortune means freedom, and I'm afraid of that. It's such a fine thing, and one should make such a use of it." (III, 320)

What Isabel needs is, if not a protector, at least a guide to that Old World she wishes to see. In Serena Merle, with her evidently vast experience and her knowledge of the ways of that world, Isabel seems to have found just such a guide. Yet the very perfection of Madame Merle's *savoir-faire* and her impeccable manners make her suspect. Isabel is just a little disturbed by this perfection, feels that her friend is not natural: "She had become too flexible, too useful, was too ripe and too final. She was in a word too perfectly the social animal. . . ." (III, 274) But she would not condemn her. At the beginning of the next chapter (Twenty), however, the unfortunate note struck by Serena's response to the news of Isabel's inheritance—"Ah . . . the clever creature!" (III, 298)—makes us the more dubious and increases our apprehension. And finally, three chapters later, when Ralph's ironic praise of Serena's virtues—"She's too good, too kind, too clever, too learned, too accomplished, too everything. She's too complete, in a word" (III, 361)—so nearly echoes Isabel's rehearsal of the unnaturalness of those virtues, we can hardly escape the feeling that her befriending Isabel is at best a mixed blessing.

That blessing seems even further mixed by Serena's introducing Isabel to Gilbert Osmond, a thoroughly Europeanized American gentleman. The effect of Gilbert on Isabel is to make her self-conscious, to make her behavior as unnatural as she had found Madame Merle's to be: on her initial visit to Osmond's villa in Florence she finds herself being more careful than she had ever been before. As her association with Osmond develops, Isabel grows more and more careful, less and less natural—much to Ralph Touchett's regret. Finally, against the wishes of almost everybody, Isabel decides to accept Osmond's proposal of marriage, for he seems to threaten her with none of the restrictive protectiveness she had feared in other proposed unions but rather to offer her the fullest opportunity of experiencing life—the life she has wanted most to see, of culture and taste and good manners. Wedded to Gilbert Osmond, she will learn what she has most needed to know.

Yet when Ralph pays his first visit to the new Mrs. Osmond, he sees the change that has been wrought, the veneer of manners that has been laid on her—but no sign of improvement. A long paragraph at the beginning of Chapter Thirty-nine carries his impressions:

> She lived with a certain magnificence, but you needed to be a member
> of her circle to perceive it; for there was nothing to gape at, nothing
> to criticize, nothing even to admire, in the daily proceedings of Mr. and
> Mrs. Osmond. Ralph, in all this, recognized the hand of the master;
> for he knew that Isabel had no faculty for producing studied impressions. (IV, 142)

And then Isabel herself appears.

> Certainly she had fallen into exaggerations—she who used to care so
> much for the pure truth. . . . Of old she had been curious, and now
> she was indifferent, and yet in spite of her indifference her activity
> was greater than ever. . . . there was an amplitude and a brilliancy
> in her personal arrangements that gave a touch of insolence to her
> beauty. Poor human-hearted Isabel, what perversity had bitten her?
> Her light step drew a mass of drapery behind it; her intelligent head
> sustained a majesty of ornament. The free, keen girl had become
> quite another person; what he saw was the fine lady who was supposed
> to represent something. What did Isabel represent? Ralph asked himself; and he could only answer by saying that she represented Gilbert
> Osmond. "Good heavens, what a function!" he then woefully exclaimed. He was lost in wonder at the eternal mystery of things.
> (IV, 143–144)

The veneer of brilliant ornament and massive drapery that has
been laid upon Isabel has had quite the same effect on her as the
convent has had on Pansy Osmond. It is not that the convent or the
drapery is in itself bad, but that they are imposed as restrictions.
Of course, Ralph's view may be biased: the stifling, muffling effect
of Osmond's influence may be all in Ralph's imagination. And it is
certain that Isabel would admit no such thing to Ralph—after all,
he had warned her and might now throw "I told you so" in her
face. Yet she is finally moved to admit it all to herself.

In Chapter Forty Isabel happens upon Osmond and Serena in a
situation apparently innocent enough, yet charged with significance.
Isabel perceives that their relationship has been of the duration
and intimacy that permits Osmond to remain seated while Serena

stands, their colloquy to lapse "into a sort of familiar silence." (IV, 164) The image of that scene stays with Isabel and sets off in her, two chapters later, a chain of ideas that serve to awaken her to the nature of her situation as Mrs. Osmond. Seated alone before the fire she reviews her life with Osmond and comes to recognize with disturbing clarity of vision how her intentions and expectations have not been realized—how awfully disappointed and perverted they have been. That recognition is expressed in terms that catch all the sense of suffocation and incarceration that her marriage has produced in her: their life "a dark, narrow alley with a dead wall at the end," (IV, 189); their dwelling "the house of darkness, the house of dumbness, the house of suffocation" (IV, 196); "it was as if Osmond deliberately, almost malignantly, had put the lights out one by one." (IV, 190) Yet she is his wife and must do what duty, according to Osmond, demands of her, and what *noblesse,* in Osmond's version of it, *oblige.*

She must suffer two more shocks of recognition, however, before her eyes are completely opened to the full horror of her situation. In spite of her marriage, Lord Warburton persists in being an attentive friend. The attentiveness, it is hoped, may spread to embrace the daughter Pansy; and thus a very advantageous marriage might result. Isabel has been urged to use her influence to move Warburton in that desirable direction. The idea does not appeal to her; but it shows in a particularly interesting light when, in a conversation between her and Serena, it is raised again. Serena's mild carelessness with pronouns quickens Isabel's sensitive suspicions. "If Lord Warburton simply got tired of the poor child, that's one thing, and it's a pity. If he gave her up to please you it's another," says Madame Merle; then she adds, "Let him off—let us have him!" As the crucial pronoun *us* burns into Isabel's consciousness she asks in horror, "What have you to do with my husband?" and then "What have you to do with me?" (IV, 326) A moment of high and terrific drama is compressed into Madame Merle's response:

> Madame Merle slowly got up, stroking her muff, but not removing her eyes from Isabel's face. "Everything!" she answered. (IV, 327)

The last blow is almost superfluous; the Countess Gemini informs Isabel that Pansy is, in a word, the illegitimate child of Gilbert and Serena. Now all is known—the truth is spelled out with all *i*'s dotted and all *t*'s crossed. "Ah, I must see Ralph!" Isabel wails. (IV, 373)

And off she flies, disobeying her husband in overt action for the very first time.

Ralph has been declining in health (most significantly) throughout Isabel's headlong career as Mrs. Osmond. He is at death's door when she arrives and lives only long enough to hear Isabel's tale of horror discovered and to tell her in return of his own boundless love for her: "if you've been hated you've also been loved. Ah but, Isabel—*adored!*" (IV, 417) At this she wants to stay with him, to die with him; but he urges her to live and assures her that she will never lose him: "You won't lose me—you'll keep me. Keep me in your heart; I shall be nearer to you than I've ever been." (IV, 413–414)

So she returns. In spite, again, of the objections of all her remaining friends, Isabel goes back to Rome, to Osmond—sadder and wiser. So this comedy, or as it is often maintained, this tragedy of manners, grinds to its conclusion.

Certain stylistic features of *The Portrait of a Lady* are important in emphasizing the structural arrangement in the novel and thus contribute to the story's significance. Isabel's career is defined, to a great extent, by the explicit opposition between Ralph Touchett and Gilbert Osmond. The terms of that opposition help to specify the values involved and to control our sympathetic responses to Isabel and her experience. To put it most simply, Ralph is responsible for Isabel's independence, as he gains for her the means of freedom; Osmond, in his turn, takes that away, assumes the burden of Isabel's inheritance, and makes her securely dependent upon him. Isabel tells herself, at the outset of Chapter Forty-five, that Osmond "wished her to have no freedom of mind, and he knew perfectly well that Ralph was an apostle of freedom." (IV, 245) One of her sharp recognitions in Chapter Forty-two was another distinction between the two men, expressed in terms of light and dark: while Osmond had made the mansion of their love a "house of darkness" by malignantly putting "the lights out one by one," Ralph's effect has been quite the opposite, for his "little visit was a lamp in the darkness." (IV, 203) Finally, the motif of flying and falling, used to describe the Icarian arc of Isabel's career from Gardencourt to Rome, qualifies our sympathetic response very effectively. The apostle of freedom early counsels Isabel to trust herself, the essential promptings of her own nature: "Don't question your conscience so much," he urges her; "Live as you like best. . . . Spread your wings; rise above the ground." (III, 319) When he makes his last attempt to dissuade

Isabel from marrying Osmond, he resorts to the same terminology. He tells her that he had planned a *high* destiny for her and that she was not to have *come down* so easily: "You seemed to me to be soaring far up in the blue—to be, sailing in the bright light, over the heads of men. Suddenly some one tosses up a faded rosebud . . . and straight you drop to the ground. It hurts me," he then adds, "hurts me as if I had fallen myself!" (IV, 69–70) And when, in her revealing reverie in Chapter Forty-two, Isabel figures her own dilemma, she too naturally employs the same terms. "Instead of leading to the high places of happiness," her marriage to Osmond "led rather downward and earthward, into realms of restriction and depression. . . ." (IV, 189)

That pattern is reflected in the fainter but broader pattern figured in the complementary progress of Osmond and Ralph in their influence on Isabel. As Gilbert succeeds, rising to the acme of his marriage to Isabel and their setting up together in "a high house in the very heart of Rome" (IV, 100), Ralph's steady decline—in health, spirits, and influence—reflects the progress of his losing cause. This complementary pattern is announced in an early scene in the novel, but so successfully embedded in the surface of the real situation as to pass almost unnoticed. At the outset of Chapter Twenty-eight Warburton goes to the opera hoping to find Isabel there and to pursue his interest with her; once arrived, he locates her in one of the boxes in an upper tier and sees Osmond up there with her. He decides to go up and join them: "He took his way to the upper regions and on the staircase met Ralph Touchett slowly descending, his hat at the inclination of ennui, and his hands where they usually were." (IV, 1–2)

These two clearly related motifs reinforce our sense of what we see happening to Isabel; they emphasize the fact that in falling away from Ralph she falls into the clutches of evil embodied in Gilbert Osmond. The quality of that evil is likewise underlined by a recurrent motif; and again it is a figurative motif artfully embedded in the very realistic details of action, setting, and dialogue. Osmond is, of course, a man of taste, of propriety, of careful manners; he holds himself well above the vulgar, superciliously looking down on almost everyone. The exception is notable: Osmond admits to having envied the Emperor of Russia and the Sultan of Turkey and "There were even moments when I envied the Pope of Rome—for the consideration he enjoys." (III, 382) Lest we miss the importance of that last, it is referred to at least twice again, most notably when Osmond comes upon Isabel in St. Peter's (Chapter Twenty-seven) and approaches her to press his attentions on her. The setting is important, and James's narrative language gently but firmly insists: "He now approached with all the forms—he appeared to have multiplied them on this occasion to suit the place." (III, 425) A few lines later she reminds him of his envy: "You ought indeed to be a Pope!" He replies, "Ah, I should have enjoyed that!" (III, 427) The occasion, the place, his reiterated envy of the Pope, all these loom larger than life. Osmond's use of the convent as a kind of cold storage for his daughter takes on added significance, as indeed do several other details—the Osmonds' dwelling in "a high house in the very heart of Rome," the city of Rome itself, and even poor Lord Warburton's sister who "had a smooth, nun-like forehead and wore a large silver cross suspended from her neck." (III, 180) And on the occasion of Osmond's most pressing proposal of marriage, when he confesses to his worship of propriety and provokes from Isabel the question "You're not conventional?" his reply speaks volumes: "No, I'm not conventional: I'm convention itself." (IV, 21)

James has used the institutions and organizations of the Roman Catholic Church as a pervasive theme to add emphasis to the most salient and sinister quality of Gilbert Osmond, the ritualistic dévoté of propriety and conventional form. It is not a condemnation of this most strictly ordered of Western institutions (we need only recall the sympathetic treatment of the two nuns who accompany Pansy at her introduction to the story in Chapter Twenty-two), but an expression of the threat involved in the misuse or abuse of convention, tradition, and manners. We have felt from the outset of the novel that Isabel's ignorance of polite conventions, of the traditions of civilized behavior, has constituted a serious lack; to be really "finished" as a complete woman, a lady—as even Isabel recognized—she needs to submit to the discipline of manners. In submitting oneself to that discipline, of course, some compromise is necessary: one's personality, one's "natural self," is necessarily circumscribed and perhaps diminished. A complete submission would mean a virtual loss of that personality, as we find in the shocking case of Pansy, who has become almost a little automaton under the discipline imposed by her father. Osmond has himself so completely surrendered his personality to the mode of manners, propriety, and good form that the adjective "conventional" is insufficient to account for him— he is convention itself, form without content. Ralph Touchett expresses it in only slightly different words:

"He's the incarnation of taste," Ralph went on, thinking hard how he could best express Gilbert Osmond's sinister attributes without putting himself in the wrong by seeming to describe him coarsely. (IV, 71)

As Osmond evilly *uses* Isabel as though she were a thing, an *objet d'art* belonging to his collection, and *uses* his daughter as though she were just such another piece in his collection to be *matched* at an opportune moment (when the market is right), we feel it is his inhumane commitment to manners alone, taste alone, the merely materialistic alone, that motivates him. He has, of course, also used Madame Merle, has made of her the perfect consort to his devilry; she is his complement and cat's paw. For as Osmond is not conventional but convention itself, so Serena is not worldly—"Worldly? No," said Ralph, "she's the great round world itself." (III, 362) Together they constitute the formidable opposition against which Ralph contends for the social and moral health of Isabel Archer. And as the novel closes with his death and Isabel's projected return to Rome and Osmond, it would seem that the victory has gone to the forces of convention, taste, and worldliness; and so some readers have sadly believed.

James has managed, by virtue of the expressive thematic network we have just been considering, to use the realistic social items of this international story as metaphoric material—to make us recognize in this account of an American girl's experience of Europe a statement about the perennial conflict between the demands of nature and the exigencies of civilized social order. The novel is, in consequence, richer, more profound and meaningful. Yet there is more.

Deeply embedded in the fabric of *The Portrait of a Lady,* stated in part in the metaphoric motifs we have reviewed and informing the very structure of the plot, there is a pattern that we can only call mythic and that is ultimately responsible for the rich resonance and profound appeal of this novel. It is simply the pattern of man's fall and redemption. The pattern is Christian, or Miltonic, or Blakean, or almost Hawthornesque. Its shape is expressed in the structural and thematic opposition of Gardencourt and Rome, in the opposition of Ralph and Osmond, and particularly in the contrast between Ralph's giving of £70.000 to Isabel and Osmond's taking Isabel (and the pounds) to himself.

Gardencourt, as its very name might suggest, has an Edenic quality. There Isabel begins her career in her full innocence; and thence she ventures out, bearing the burden of Ralph's gift of freedom, to face her experience in the world. The opening paragraph of the novel describes Gardencourt in suggestive terms. The scene opens on "the perfect middle of a splendid summer afternoon" at teatime, "on certain occasions a little eternity; but on such an occasion as this . . . an eternity of pleasure." And it is in the very heart of Rome that Isabel, having learned to be self-conscious, to subdue her natural spontaneity, to try to be a dutiful wife, dwells with her husband and under his dominance. She has been victimized by his evil, his "emotional cannibalism," which is defined as specifically diabolical by the terms of Isabel's recognition of her predicament. She has been deceived by the beautiful veneer of Osmond's manners, but now sees the depth of evil beneath: "Under all his culture, his cleverness, his amenity, under his good-nature, his facility, his knowledge of life, his egotism lay hidden like a serpent in a bank of flowers." (IV, 196) He is the classic image of the Satanic figure of evil in the garden. And it is to this that Isabel is wedded.

Such a commitment has deprived Isabel of her innocence and her freedom—as commitment to evil always does: "But for the money [£70.000] as she saw to-day, she would never have done it. . . . At bottom her money had been a burden. . . ." (IV, 192–193) Typically, poor human-hearted Isabel has found the responsibility of freedom too great a burden to bear alone and unsupported and, again typically, has transferred the weight of that burden to the one who is most willing to accept it—not to share the load but to remove it completely. All this Isabel recognizes, though as yet somewhat imperfectly. Her essential nature prompts her to turn then for help to her original sponsor, the unselfish Ralph. In Chapter Forty-five they discuss the possible match between Pansy and Warburton, so avidly desired by Osmond and Serena; and Isabel is trying to be the dutiful wife and contribute to the *catching* of Warburton, but is troubled by the question of whom Warburton really loves. At a crucial moment in the discussion, " 'Ah, Ralph, you give me no help!' she cried abruptly and passionately." She immediately regrets it. "It was the first time she had alluded to the need for help, and the words shook her cousin with their violence. He gave a long murmur of relief, of pity, of tenderness; it seemed to him that at last the gulf between them had been bridged." (IV, 249) But it is not the last. When she is granted full vision by the Countess Gemini's finishing touches to the sordid tale of Gilbert, Serena, and Pansy, Isabel's immediate response is, we recall, "Ah, I must see Ralph!" (IV, 373).

Clearly enough, her choice of Osmond has meant her rejection of Ralph. Commitment to Osmond has meant, Isabel recognizes in Chapter Forty-two, commitment to "this base, ignoble world . . . ; one was to keep it forever in one's eye, in order not to enlighten it or convert or redeem it, but to extract from it some recognition of one's superiority." (IV, 197) Ralph has been characterized throughout as the epitome of unworldliness. His hold on this world, by the nature of his health, has been most precarious. He has been repeatedly associated, jocularly, with the unsubstantial, with the air. His reason for getting the bequest of £70.000 for Isabel, he said, was that he wanted "to put a little wind in her sails" (III, 260); at the end of Chapter Thirty-four (after a lengthy attempt at dissuading Isabel from accepting Osmond) Isabel urges him to join her for breakfast, "You ought to eat . . . you live on air"—he agrees, "I do very much, and I shall go back into the garden and take another mouthful." (IV, 75) Much later, when Ralph has decided to leave Rome and return to England, Isabel pays him one of her infrequent visits and is surprised at his saying that he has heard a great deal about her— "From the voices of the air! Oh, from no one else. . . ." (IV, 305)

Then there is his odd association with the ghost of Gardencourt. When the worst is known, it is to Ralph and the promising shelter of Gardencourt that Isabel wishes to fly. She had thought, at the moment of Ralph's proposed departure for England, that there was "something sacred in Gardencourt"; she adds, significantly, "no chapter of the past was more perfectly irrecoverable." (IV, 296) And when at last she is herself on her way back, she thinks "Gardencourt had been her starting-point, and to those muffled chambers it was at least a temporary solution to return. She had gone forth in her strength; she would come back in her weakness, and if the place had been a rest to her before it would be a sanctuary now." (IV, 391) The vocabulary—"sacred" and "sanctuary"—picks up faint echoes from the initial passage of the novel describing the perfection of the "little eternity" of teatime at Gardencourt, and adds the extra, mythic dimension to give it an Edenic quality. That quality is emphasized by Isabel's recognition that the Gardencourt chapter is "perfectly irrecoverable," and that to return there is a *temporary* solution. These references to Gardencourt suggest, further, something like the completing of a pattern: there was her starting-point, thither she might now return—temporarily.

Both of these aspects—the significance of the sacred and Edenic quality of Gardencourt and its importance in the pattern of Isabel's career—stand out in the closing chapters of the novel. In the account of her journey back to England, James has insisted on the wasteland atmosphere through which Isabel travels: "she performed her journey with sightless eyes and took little pleasure in the countries she traversed, decked though they were in the richest freshness of spring."

> Her thoughts followed their course through other countries—strange-looking, dimly-lighted, pathless lands, in which there was no change of seasons, but only, as it were, a perpetual dreariness of winter. . . . She envied Ralph his dying, for if one were thinking of rest that was the most perfect of all. To cease utterly, to give it all up and not know anything more—this idea was sweet as the vision of a cool bath, in a darkened chamber, in a hot land.
>
> She had moments indeed in her journey from Rome which were almost as good as being dead. (IV, 390–391)

Arriving at Gardencourt, she finds its irrecoverability in a sense confirmed: "Mrs. Osmond was a stranger; so that instead of being conducted to her own apartment she was coldly shown into the drawing-room and left to wait. . . ." (IV, 403) Furthermore, she is unable to see Ralph at first. She enquires about his condition, asking whether there is any hope. Mrs. Touchett admits flatly that there is none whatever and adds the strange comment, "There never has been." (IV, 405) With the other peculiar features of Ralph's characterization, this last comment is striking—as though it had been said of him "He's not long for this world," and now is said "He never has been." The world has never been his—nor he its! Isabel does get to see Ralph, but there is virtually no communication: "he lay three days in a kind of grateful silence. . . . Ralph, however, spoke at last—on the evening of the third day." (IV, 411–412) The significance of the three-day interval strikes us now with peculiar force, reminding us inevitably of another three-day interval in the career of one whose death was intended to save us from the grasp of supreme evil—even as Ralph's failing and death serve to draw Isabel out of the grasp of Osmond. In each case the full effect of the sacrifice depends on its acceptance—one need only admit his need and ask that it be for him. *That* Isabel is now able to do. She recognizes and expresses her gratitude to Ralph, and begs him pathetically not to leave her. Then he makes that telling reply—"Keep me in your heart"—that we cannot forget. Isabel opens her heart to Ralph and spills all her grief. He assures her that he has always known, always

understood, implying that he has always been there to help her
had she but asked. "You were ground in the very mill of the conventional!" he says pointedly. (IV, 415) His last, touching word to
her is an assurance of his love—"Ah but, Isabel—*adored!*" With
that Ralph has given up, as we say, the ghost.

We recognize in Ralph the son of the father who was ultimately
the source of Isabel's freedom, the son who was instrumental in con-
veying that gift; and finally it is Ralph's death that is the means
of freeing Isabel from the grasp of evil. In leaving Rome to return
to Gardencourt, Isabel committed her first positive action against
Osmond's wishes. But still the novel has another touch to add to its
mythic pattern. The final chapter opens with a reference to the
early chapter in which Isabel has expressed her wish to see the
ghost of Gardencourt; Ralph has told her that while he might show
it to her, she would be unable to see it, that it could never be seen
by "a young, happy innocent person like you." In order to see the
ghost, he explained, one must have suffered, have gained "some
miserable knowledge." (III, 64) Isabel has now unmistakably
gained those qualifications, and as Ralph dies she apparently is
granted her vision. Here is the account, with its significantly ambiguous pronouns:

> He had told her . . . that if she should live to suffer enough she
> might some day see the ghost with which the old house was duly pro-
> vided. She apparently had fulfilled the necessary condition; for the
> next morning, in the cold, faint dawn she knew that a spirit was stand-
> ing by her bed. She [believed] . . . that Ralph would not outlast the
> night. . . . at the time the darkness began vaguely to grow grey she
> started up from her pillow as abruptly as if she had received a sum-
> mons. It seemed to her for an instant that he was standing there—a
> vague, hovering figure in the vagueness of the room. She started a
> moment; she saw his white face—his kind eyes; then she saw there
> was nothing. She was not afraid; she was only sure. (IV, 418)

Ralph and the ghost are closely associated, almost confused. And if
there is a sacredness, a holiness about Gardencourt, there is also
about its ghost; and there is, thus, a Pentecostal dimension to that
scene, which opens the final chapter. It recalls with new significance,
therefore, that early passage in which Ralph expresses his wish to
play an *inspirational* role in Isabel's life—to put wind in her sails!

The mythic pattern of man's fall and salvation—in terms of
Isabel's departure from Gardencourt, her yielding to Osmond and

giving up her freedom, her recognition of her association with evil, her accepting the opportunity that Ralph's dying affords her, and with it his undying love—is thus complete and hopefully quite discernible in the very fabric of the story's surface. This does not take us to the very end of the novel, but it does make that end clearly understandable—and as gratefully satisfactory as the sensitive reader has already felt it to be.

If Isabel's career has taken her from the state of innocence deep into the world of experience, where she has seen the evil of that world but yet the goodness beyond, it has led her to that ultimate state described by William Blake as "higher innocence," or the state of man after salvation. The question remains: what then does such a person do? The only possible answer is already available in Isabel's own language of Chapter Forty-two: one turns to face "this base ignoble world . . . to enlighten or convert or redeem it. . . ." Inspired and strengthened by knowledge and love, one does what one must.

Thus Isabel returns to Rome and to Osmond. She has been through the valley of the shadow and has lost her life in order to find it. She asserted her independence of Osmond by leaving, against his express wishes, to see Ralph. She will not be returning to *the same situation*, for she herself has changed. She returns to Rome out of no sense of duty to Osmond but out of duty to herself—to that self, no longer merely innocent, naïve, uninformed, but fully knowing, experienced, informed with the *generous* love of Ralph, a self on which she can now safely rely.

Henrietta Stackpole has helped us, through her fond but well-meant urging, to recognize this development in Isabel. Just before Ralph's departure from Rome she urges Isabel to leave Osmond. "I can't change that way," Isabel answered her. She does not say that she could not change, but simply that she could not change *that way*. To make sure that we catch the emphasis, James has Isabel repeat it a dozen lines later, altered only to give it a broader, general application: " 'One can't change that way,' Isabel repeated." (IV, 284) Once in England, Isabel faces more urging, this time not to return to Rome. She tells Henrietta she has promised Pansy she would return, but adds that she is not sure she now sees why she made that promise.

"If you've forgotten your reason perhaps you won't return."
Isabel waited a moment. "Perhaps I shall find another." (IV, 398)

We see that Isabel, free of Osmond, has both courage and hope: she is not willing to take the easy and available way out, but is proving herself at last ready for the responsibility that real freedom demands. She looks for a meaningful change in herself that will enable her to discover the real and valid reason to return and face the world. The change and the reason come finally at Gardencourt with Ralph, from whom she at last receives the pledge of undying · and uncontingent love.

The last test, which has presented a problem to many critics of the novel, is supplied by Caspar Goodwood. He makes his last attempt to win Isabel, shrewdly striking when she is apparently most vulnerable, most susceptible. What he offers her is unmistakable; and what can we call it but love?—and with that very attractive (let us make no mistake!) love, his care and protection. Goodwood's qualities are likewise unmistakable—his name is suggestive of some of them; we know he is a "manager of men," and his general appearance —with Dick Tracy jaw (III, 164–165)—fully expresses the masculinity that is poignantly designated by the string of adjectives applied to him at the outset of Chapter Thirty-two—straight, strong, and hard. (IV, 43) That maleness asserts itself again at the close of the novel, and Isabel is fully sensible of its appeal. She responds to his kiss "like white lightning," but wrenches herself free. (IV, 436) Her refusal of Caspar has been mistakenly interpreted as a sign of her fear of sexual involvement. The very opposite is true. She had known that intimacy at first with Osmond ("the first year of their life together [was] so admirably intimate at first" [IV, 190]), and clearly responds to this advance of Caspar's. The point is that Isabel has seen the light and recognized what she must do; she has refused other escapes and evasions, and this last temptation from Caspar— so easy to yield to—would also be an escape, and a delicious one at that. But to accomplish her end, to face life as she now knows she has to, she must not turn aside but go directly ahead. (We shall find the same temptation similarly refused in *The Golden Bowl*: Maggie realizes that to win her husband back completely she must pursue the line of action she has adopted, must force her moment to its crisis, and must therefore not be swayed from her purpose by Amerigo's terribly attractive sexual advances.) The paragraph in which Caspar has so tellingly kissed Isabel ends with two resonant sentences. "She had not known where to turn; but she knew now. There was a very straight path." (IV, 436)

The Portrait of a Lady is not tragic. Part of its convincing realism lies in its refusal to promise a happy ending, or to suggest even that accepting the "right way" brings happiness. But it can bring satisfaction and indeed the only freedom humanity can know. It is a freedom that comes from a refusal to submit to the dominance of the merely worldly, of the exigencies of the "mind-forged manacles," and from a willingness to embrace the guidance of the force of love in whose service lies perfect freedom. That Isabel has found. With that her portrait is complete.

OTHER STORIES OF THE MIDDLE YEARS

During the two decades following the publication of *The Portrait of a Lady* the international theme is absent from James's major fiction, but it does appear in several short stories of that period. Those stories are, in general, much nearer the mode of comedy of manners and social satire than are the earlier stories. In "The Siege of London" (1883), for example, we have something like an older and shrewder and much-married and divorced Daisy Miller in the person of the determined heroine Mrs. Headway, who relentlessly lays her siege to the social world of London and finally forces her way—through marriage with a rather spineless equivalent of Lord Lambeth, Sir Arthur Demesne.

Two interesting exceptions that use the international theme are "The Pupil" (1891) and "Europe" (1899). The earlier of these is concerned exclusively with Americans in Europe: the rather down-at-heel Moreen family ("a houseful of Bohemians who wanted tremendously to be Philistines")[13] and a naïve American student from Oxford whom they engage as tutor for their sensitive and precocious son Morgan. The story is especially worth our attention because of its central relationship between the tutor, Pemberton, and his pupil; it resembles the relationship between Isabel Archer and Ralph Touchett in the *Portrait* and anticipates that between Merton Densher and Milly Theale in *The Wings of the Dove*. Pemberton needs the money that the position of tutor with the Moreens promises, so he applies for the job. He is impressed by the European experience of the Moreens (his own has been rather limited) and amazed by what he takes to be their sophistication; he is convinced that "living with them would really be to see life" (XI, 519):

[13] *Novels and Tales*, XI, 521; subsequent references are in the text.

They talked of "good places" as if they had been pickpockets or strolling players. They had at Nice a villa, a carriage, a piano and a banjo, and they went to official parties. (XI, 520)

He has accepted the job of tutor, although Mrs. Moreen has left the pecuniary terms of his employment quite vague. In fact they do not pay him, and go so far as to suggest that he is amply rewarded by his pleasant relationship with their charming son. Pemberton thus finds out about the evil of the world, especially that of the wretched manipulation and use of human beings as though they were objects of barter. Little Morgan, who is no more robust in health than Ralph or Milly Theale, knows his family and its ways all too well and from the first urges Pemberton not to stay, but cannot convince him that they really are rotters: "They're so beastly worldly. That's what I hate most . . . ! All they care about is to make an appearance and to pass for something or other." (XI, 549) An opportunity for the great escape of Pemberton and Morgan together occurs when the flimsy family fortunes have apparently worn through: the parents are obviously chucking things overboard to try to save the ship in this storm (the metaphor is James's) and want to unload Morgan onto Pemberton. Morgan is of course delighted: here is the chance to get away from parents who love him no more than a trinket and to join with a tutor who does care for him. Pemberton is only embarrassed, or afraid he will be with Morgan's frail life on his hands, and hesitates to take up the Moreens' offer. The shock of Pemberton's tacit refusal is more than Morgan's weak heart can stand: Morgan suffers, like all those who are not loved, from "heart trouble." He dies. His dying serves, however, to free Pemberton definitely once and for all from the clutches of the Moreens. But Morgan has not the time to tell Pemberton to keep him in his heart—as Ralph does Isabel. It seems, however, as though Pemberton has indeed kept him in his heart, or at least in his thoughts: "Today, after a considerable interval," Pemberton is still cherishing his "few tangible tokens—a lock of Morgan's hair cut by his own hand, and the half-dozen letters received from him when they were disjoined." (XI, 518) And perhaps he has benefited from the lesson Morgan helped him learn about emotional cannibals and their purely worldly considerations.

"Europe" is set in America and concerns almost exclusively the widowed mother and three daughters of the Rimmle family and the

narrator. Mrs. Rimmle is incredibly ancient; and her daughters, well
on the way to becoming old maids, are strictly obedient and even
docile—with the exception of Jane. The story is a development of
the idea of the "great American disease"—the affliction of Caroline
Spencer—in a rather perverse way. Mrs. Rimmle has been to Europe
with her husband years ago and she dangles that experience before
her daughters like the promise of the pearly gates. It is their great
topic of conversation and study, for it is understood that the girls
are to go, two of them, when their mother's health permits. When-
ever plans are about settled for the girls' departure, Mrs. Rimmle
suffers a relapse, which absolutely exasperates the narrator (the
typical Jamesian narrator, an inveterate transatlantic traveler) but
hardly discomfits the girls—with the exception of Jane. She grasps
the opportunity of going to Europe on the invitation of the Hathaways; and she will not return. The Hathaways come back without
her. As the narrator puts it, with Maria's prompting, Jane has
"tasted blood." [14] It sounds a bit bestial, but the point is that Jane
is at last really seeing life—the blood she tastes is, so to speak,
like the blood spilled on Lucy Honeychurch's postcards of Florence
in E. M. Forster's *A Room with a View*. Mrs. Rimmle has grown
senile and with her daughter's refusal to return affects to believe that
Jane is dead, and so reports to the narrator. The complementary twist
in James's exposure of this odd disease is that when the second
daughter does in fact die, Mrs. Rimmle insists that she is not dead
but has gone to Europe. The dominant irony of the story is that
while real life awaits the Rimmle girls—and anyone else—in Europe,
the controlling view, that is Mrs. Rimmle's, is that real life is in
America and life in Europe is—what shall we say—*heavenly* or
dreamlike or otherworldly and in any case *not real*.

"Pandora" (1884) deserves a word if only because it is the other
side of the Daisy Miller coin—quite explicitly so. Pandora Day is
Daisy safely in America, but not safe from the satiric exposure to
which James subjects her. He uses the foreign eye of Count Vogelstein, who has crossed on the ship bringing Pandora back from a
sojourn in Europe as he is coming to join the German legation in
Washington. The world of American society and American politics
appears, in Vogelstein's baleful view, to be a culturally deprived area.
The satire is reflexive, however—as it is in the opening sections of

[14] *Novels and Tales,* XVI, 359.

"An International Episode"—so that Vogelstein is satirized in his turn by his view of America. He has learned about the bizarre species, the American *jeune fille*, from reading "Daisy Miller."

Much of James's energy and interest during the eighties were devoted to trying his hand at adapting the mode of French Naturalism to his own style of writing, not simply increased attention to accurate and detailed representation of characters and setting, but an attempt to write fiction that examined the influence of heredity and environment in determining the fate of his characters. Some of the international stories show evidence of this preoccupation with Zolaesque *experimental* fiction. "Lady Barberina" (1884) is a good example. While it demonstrates, typically, the difficulty of achieving successful compromise between European and American, the antagonistic forces are not simply European manners and American *morals:* the suggestion here is that the two are *congenitally* incapable of accommodating each other—that the problems arise from deep-seated and long-standing differences. The story concerns the attempt of a wealthy young American physician, Jackson Lemon, to achieve a successful marriage with the Lady Barberina (spelled "Barbarina" in the New York Edition), a daughter of the Cantervilles, an aristocratic English family—and to introduce her into his native milieu. Lemon has been warned of the difficulty of such a venture, and he gets some sense of what is involved as he contemplates his intended bride: "she seemed to him to have a part of the history of England in her blood; she was the fine flower of generations of privileged people, and of centuries of rich country-life." [15] Lemon is not faced with the prospect that confronted Christopher Newman, of learning the manners and acquiring the taste and living into the traditions of the European society; what Lemon faces is something in the Canterville heritage, inborn and firmly rooted in the past and in the family genes—or so the story's emphasis makes us feel. For his part, Jackson is by no means the bear, the social misfit that Newman was; but he comes out of the same tradition. He has the strong will, the stout self-confidence, the democratic conviction of his own worth as second to none. As James puts it, Jackson is "heir of all the ages." (XIV, 86) A true son of America, he is cousin to Daisy Miller—but infinitely more intelligent than she. The first test for Lemon comes with the Cantervilles' insistence that the marriage settlement be arranged between their solicitors. At once Jackson gets his back up:

---

[15] *Novels and Tales,* XIV, 74; subsequent references are in the text.

not that he does not intend to provide generously for his wife, but he objects to being obliged to do so and chafes at what he feels is legal pressure. Other tests follow with distressing regularity. Lady Barb is rigidly unhappy in America—no compromise possible there; Jackson reluctantly removes with his wife to Europe. He has triumphed in gaining his aristocratic wife, but has not been able to domesticate her: an empty success. The failure of the attempted compromise is due, we are tempted to say, to the natures of Barb and Jackson; yet we cannot escape the feeling that the responsible forces are beneath, long-sired and deeply laid; and we can almost agree with Jackson's notion that, despite all, you cannot "change the nature of things." (XIV, 136)

Somewhat different purposes are at work in stories like "Lady Barberina" even though they deal familiarly with the international theme. The theme as we have been accustomed to it is resumed with the turn of the century, and reappears in his novels.

THE MAJOR PHASE

In the opening years of the twentieth century James published in regular annual succession three substantial and important novels on the international theme—*The Wings of the Dove, The Ambassadors,* and *The Golden Bowl.* These are the three great novels of what has come to be called his "major phase"; and they resume the theme that had been absent from his novels for over twenty years, and in doing so demonstrate a considerable technical advance and a notable maturing of attitude. The germinal ideas from which these novels grew date from the middle of the 1890s, or immediately after the theatrical experiment that ended with the fiasco of *Guy Domville.* All three show the advantage of that experiment to the development of James's narrative technique, as all three express the careers of the respective heroes in theatrical and dramatic terms.

The first of the three, *The Wings of the Dove,* was published in 1902. The first note for the novel, however, appears in James's Notebooks under the date November 3, 1894, and even then looks further back. Just when James thought the idea came to him is not clear, but it must have been with him ever since the death in 1870 of his beloved cousin, Minny Temple. Much later, in writing *Notes of a Son and Brother* (1914), he pays fond tribute to Minny, recalling the tragic nature of early death of one so eager to live: "I was in the far-off aftertime to seek to lay the ghost by wrapping it, a particular occasion aiding, in the beauty and dignity of art." [16] Minny Temple thus *became* Milly Theale.

But the line of descent was not immediate. In 1884 James published an indifferent short story called "Georgina's Reasons." It is a rather improbable tale of the secret marriage of Georgina to a naval officer, Benyon. After long separation Georgina contracts another and therefore bigamous marriage; Benyon in turn falls in love a second time and returns to Georgina to demand that their marriage be acknowledged so that it may be dissolved. Georgina refuses and Benyon is obliged to await her pleasure. The strong-willed Georgina is rather like Kate Croy in *Wings*, and what encourages us to think of that comparison a moment is the late appearance in "Georgina's Reason's" of two sisters—Kate and Milly Theory—with one of whom Benyon has fallen in love. Milly Theory is an invalid, as Milly Theale is in failing health in *Wings*, and is described as being "as beautiful as a saint, and as delicate and refined as an angel." [17] Benyon's situation between Georgina and the Theory girl, committed by legal bonds to the one and by love to the other, is in its essence like Densher's situation between Kate Croy and Milly Theale in the closing chapters of *The Wings of the Dove*.

The center of attention in the novel is, of course, Milly Theale. She is again the young American heroine of whom James was so fond. Besides being typically innocent and naïve and eager to live, she is a gentle creature without those abrasive edges that characterize even the most attractive of her predecessors. Furthermore, she is fabulously wealthy—although in calling her "the potential heiress of all the ages" [18] James meant to refer to more than her immense material inheritance (even as he did in similarly designating Jackson Lemon in "Lady Barberina"). With this she is starkly independent, quite without family. This combination of features, and especially her genial gentleness, her extreme wealth, and her lack of family, makes her a particularly vulnerable prey to the predators with whom she comes into contact in Europe. If she is a "princess," as the novel calls her (XIX, 120)—to emphasize her personal value as well as her wealth—she is also the dove of the novel's title, as the story reminds us repeatedly—to suggest her softness and gentleness and purity, but

---

[16] *Autobiography*, p. 544.
[17] *Tales*, VI, 45.
[18] *Novels and Tales*, XIX, 109; subsequent references are in the text.

also (therefore) to express the appropriateness and worth of the sacrifice she becomes at the close of the book.

For the novel's central concern is much like that of *The Portrait of a Lady:* the insufficiency of the American *naïve* in her confrontation with the heavily civilized world of Europe. Milly, like Isabel, is a ready victim of the fine-mannered schemers who dazzle and delude her. That society is impressively represented by Aunt Maud Lowder and Lord Mark and the general way of life at Lancaster Gate. The facet of the life that emerges most sharply is the meanly and crassly mercantile standard of value. Our first view of the solid and substantial Aunt Maud reveals her as "Britannia of the Market Place—Britannia unmistakable but with a pen in her ear." She is called, further, "unscrupulous and immoral." (XIX, 30–31) If she is therefore a threatening figure, Kate Croy asks herself (it is Kate's view of her aunt) what the dangers are but just the dangers of life and of London: "Mrs. Lowder *was* London, *was* life—the roar of the siege and the thick of the fray." (XIX, 32) It is a world that does not pretend to know what people are for, but only what they are worth and what can be done with them. Into that world flutters the fabulously rich and innocent Milly Theale, eager for life but threatened with early death. Of course she does not understand that world, for Mrs. Lowder's life bristled, for her, with unfamiliar elements: "They represented . . . the world, the world that, as a consequence of the cold shoulder turned to it by the Pilgrim Fathers, had never yet boldly crossed to Boston." (XIX, 170)

The mercantile avidity soon enough turns itself to Milly, as Kate and Merton decide to make use of her for their own happiness. But while Kate and Merton are the immediate agents of the evil directed at Milly, the novel carefully refrains from turning them into melodramatic villains, carefully retains our sympathy and understanding for them. Kate has been indoctrinated from an early age by her father to consider herself as a marketable item; he has impressed on her conscience the idea that her duty is to cash in on herself at Lancaster Gate for the general benefit of her family. Aunt Maud is interested in her handsome niece and also is aware of Kate's market value; she agrees to keep her at Lancaster Gate. A complication is Kate's love for Merton Densher: they cannot marry because of lack of money, though they hope ultimately to win Aunt Maud's favor and cash blessing. Their hope is dim, however, as Aunt Maud explains to Merton early in Chapter Four. The idiom of the explanation is significant:

". . . Kate's presence—unluckily for *you*—is everything I could possibly wish . . . and I've been keeping it for the comfort of my declining years. I've watched it long; I've been saving it up and letting it, as you say of investments, appreciate, and you may judge whether, now it has begun to pay so, I'm likely to treat for it with any but a high bidder. I can do the best with her and I've my idea of the best." (XIX, 82)

Her idea is a title, and Lord Mark can thus make the high bid and is glad to do so (Kate will have a generous dowry from her Aunt Maud)—until the genial clink of Milly Theale's shekels distracts him.

Trained in this way Kate naturally enough concocts her plan of marrying Merton to Milly and then herself marrying the wealthy widower he will become on Milly's imminent death. Merton is even more the victim of the force of cupidity and hence more sympathetic than Kate. Lancaster Gate keeps him from his love and he understandably hates all the elements of which that world is composed: they "represented for him a portentous negation of his own world of thought." (XIX, 79) But his love of Kate draws him on and finally commits him—at least temporarily—to the system and values of Lancaster Gate. He bargains for love. His response to Kate's plan to get Milly's millions is to ask Kate to "come to him" in his rooms. He too sees Kate's market value; Kate herself knows what the exchange rate has to be: "I'll come," she promises him, and thereby enlists herself in the oldest profession in the world. (XX, 231)

Milly is the prize they are all after—the dearest in the eyes of cupidity. She is a valuable thing, yet her apparent tragedy is that with all her vulnerable virtues she is unprepared to cope with London and the world. Not only is she to die but she is to suffer and be touched where the suffering will be most acute—in her love. It is her early and obvious attraction to Merton, coupled with the revelation of her severely limited expectancy, that has prompted Kate to hatch her marriage plot. The general insensitivity of the other characters to Milly's exposed humanity is given added emphasis of expression by one of the principal figurative motifs in the story.

Milly is supposed to resemble a Bronzino portrait. Lord Mark asks her if she has seen it, "the beautiful one that's so like you?" (XIX, 217) Here, at the beginning of Chapter Eleven, she and Lord Mark approach it together, and Milly is glad of his attendance, his obvious wish to take care of her a little; she feels, indeed, that that is what "all the people with the kind eyes were wishing" (XIX,

220)—the crowd of his London friends, including Kate and Aunt Maud, who are watching them. But confronting the portrait Milly sees that it is of "a very great personage—only unaccompanied by a joy. And she was dead, dead, dead." Her comment is puzzling to Lord Mark, but redolent with significance: "I shall never be better than this." (XIX, 221) He mistakes her outburst for modesty; she tries to correct his understanding by insisting that she does not see the resemblance—affirming that her complexion is several times greener, her hands several times larger than those of the figure in the portrait. Poor Milly is attempting to make him and the others see that she is really something *more* than a portrait—more than a representative surface—and alive, not dead, dead, dead. She has had a fearful glimpse of the truth that for them, the world of Lancaster Gate, she will indeed "never be better than" the Bronzino portrait. For it is a world, we recognize with Milly, that attends to surfaces, to what meets the eye, and that is all too liable to treat all lovely and high-priced things equally—equally as *things*.

But Milly has herself participated in that error to some extent, as is frequently the case with the Jamesian hero. She herself has tended to look at life—at least at life in Europe—as though it were contained within a frame or, sometimes, placed behind footlights. Book Fourth opens on a scene at dinner at Lancaster Gate; Milly notices all the guests, but especially the Bishop of Murrum, "a real bishop," with "a complicated costume . . . and a face all the portrait of a prelate." (XIX, 147) The scene in general, all its rich and romantic details, "were all touches in a picture and denotements in a play." (XIX, 148) Book Fifth reiterates the motif, as we learn that the great historic house strikes Milly as "the centre of an almost extravagantly grand Watteau-composition." (XIX, 208) Almost inevitably, then, after the Bronzino episode Milly sees herself taking her place in this world in terms of being hung in a gallery: "she should be as one of the circle of eminent contemporaries, photographed, engraved, signatured, and in particular framed and glazed, who made up the rest of the decoration." (XIX, 237)

The picture motif reaches its significant conclusion at the end of the novel—after Kate and Densher's scheme has been foiled by Lord Mark's malevolent revelation of it to Milly—when Densher is struck with the full realization of the evil to which Milly has been subjected by them all. In the closing pages of Book Ninth Merton finds himself "in presence of the truth that was truest about Milly" (XX,

298): her existence for them all had been ringed about by smiles and silences and beautiful fictions. The suggestion is partly that they behaved *for* her as though everything (and especially, of course, her health) were all right; but it is also that they had behaved to keep *all* truth from her. In everything they had blinked the real. "It was a conspiracy of silence, as the *cliché* went, to which no one had made an exception, the great smudge of mortality across the picture, the shadow of pain and horror, finding in no quarter a surface of spirit or of speech that consented to reflect it." He attributes the general failure to "The mere aesthetic instinct of mankind," and curses them all for living fearfully in a fool's paradise—"the outrage even to taste involved in one's having to *see*." (XX, 298–299) But Densher at last does see, and the truth he sees is the reality—the mortality—of the subject of the "picture." His realization awakens the echo of Susan Stringham's initial impression of Milly, at the opening of Book Third, as "the real thing" and "the great reality." (XX, 105, 109) And with Densher we realize that what Milly is and represents in the novel is indeed the truly real.

In the second half of the novel the center of interest shifts to a considerable extent from Milly to Merton Densher. We continue to be concerned with Milly's welfare and what the "world" will do to her, but we become increasingly concerned with Merton's concern over her fate and his role in determining it. Thus, his realization of the truth that was truest about Milly marks a climactic moment in the novel, and turns out to be his virtual salvation.

Merton does not begin like the typical hero of James's international stories in perfect innocence; yet he has previously been in touch, so to speak, with innocence during an early visit to America when he met Milly Theale. But he is at the outset largely untainted by the corruption that lurks in Lancaster Gate. He loves Kate Croy for the goodness in her that has itself not yet been completely spoiled by that corruption. As he necessarily becomes more intimately involved with that world, which holds Kate, his love for her becomes tainted and its value changes; it threatens to become mere cupidity and concupiscence. He and Kate then revel in their "physical felicity"; and that felicity reaches its culmination in the act of virtual prostitution that Merton demands of her to seal the bargain. That act is the equivalent of Isabel Archer's marriage in *The Portrait of a Lady:* Merton has yielded to the temptation of the force that rules at Lancaster Gate—the inhuman *use* of human beings. Now he in turn can be made use of for the evil end of getting Milly's riches.

His experience of Milly, as he pays his pretended court to her, touches him more deeply than anyone had anticipated. Finally his attention to Milly pulls him out, willy-nilly, of his commitment to Kate and the values of the materialistic world she has come to represent. And Milly obviously has seen in Merton value that can be redeemed and is well worth saving—even though Lord Mark has exposed him. Merton is still the beneficiary of Milly's love, in the tangible token of her bequest and, most significantly, in her memory. In spite of his stated willingness to return to Kate, after Milly's death, and resume relations "as we were," Kate sees quite clearly the impossibility of that, sees that all is changed. Although Merton denies his love for Milly, Kate again contradicts him with the truth: "Her memory's your love. You *want* no other." (XX, 405)

If *The Wings of the Dove* closely resembles *The Portrait of a Lady* in theme, it is dangerously similar in technique to *The American*. To insist, as the novel obviously does, on the dovelike quality of Milly Theale is to risk "descending" into mere allegory, especially when that dovelike creature is the means of redeeming what is redeemable in this world, of saving Merton Densher—and probably Kate, too—from ultimate commitment to the merely material and simply physical; and even more, when the token of her lasting love was timed to arrive on Christmas Eve. To insist any further would be to state flatly that Milly Theale = the Holy Ghost. So close, indeed, does the novel verge on allegory that some fearful critics have denied the obvious similarity between Milly's role in the novel and that of the Holy Ghost in the Christian myth. They explain, with ready quotation, James's express dislike of allegory. One can only reply that James, then, did not want this novel to be allegorical and maybe did not even want Milly to be the Paraclete. But some such association there visibly *is* in the novel, and that association stresses this novel's similarity to *The Portrait of a Lady*. What James *intended*, finally, may be a purely academic (or New Critical) question. It is perfectly apparent, however, that if he did not intend Milly and Ralph to equal *the* Paraclete, he did intend them to resemble a paraclete—his own favorite, Minny Temple. A few passages from his long letter to his brother William on the occasion of Minny's death are peculiarly relevant.

Among the sad reflections that her death provokes for me, there is none sadder than this view of the gradual change and reversal of our relations: I slowly crawling from weakness and inaction and suffering into strength and health and hope: she sinking out of brightness and youth into decline and death. It's almost as if [Note!] she had passed away—as far as I am concerned—from having served her purpose, that of standing well within the world, inviting and inviting me onward by all the bright intensity of her example.[19]

In terms particularly illuminating for our consideration of the international theme, James continued, "She was a breathing protest against English grossness, English compromises and conventions—a plant of pure American growth." [20] And perhaps most significant of all is this elegiac note of optimisitic faith:

> What once was life is always life, in one form or another, and speaking simply of this world I feel as if in effect and influence Minny had lost very little by her change of state. She lives as a steady unfaltering luminary in the mind rather than as a flickering wasting earth-stifled lamp.[21]

That is quite the note sounded in *The Wings of the Dove*—"Her memory's your love. You *want* no other."—and in *The Portrait of a Lady*—"You won't lose me, you'll keep me. Keep me in your heart. . . ."

This allegorical element has to be wrenched out, for fully discrete visibility, from the thick bed of the metaphor in which it is fixed in the novel. And that metaphor of the international theme expresses in *Wings* very much the same idea that it does elsewhere in James's fiction. The American figure of innocent purity embodies its familiar virtues and exposes its insufficiencies for existence in this world. It is thrust into immediate contact with the experienced world of Europe, which embodies the mundane threat and dangers but also the taste and the sense of manners that make civilization possible. Here in *Wings*, as elsewhere, the paramount evil of "emotional cannibalism" is defined and the importance of full consciousness, clear vision, and spiritual love to the hero's salvation is emphasized. The polarity is nicely expressed, and we feel the novel's yearning for compromise, for resolution of the opposites. Typically, the Jamesian international story seems to be striving to achieve the *successful* union of the American and European figures (usually in marriage);

[19] Quoted in F. O. Matthiessen, *The James Family* (New York: Alfred A. Knopf, 1947), pp. 260–261.
[20] *James Family*, p. 263.
[21] *James Family*, p. 262.

and typically the story stops short of realizing such a union. In *Wings,* Densher is torn between love for Kate and love for Milly; the impossible resolution would provide him with a partner who combined the two—a Milly Croy, a Kate Theale. Or perhaps *Wings,* like the *Portrait,* points beyond itself to a glorious tomorrow in which Merton can marry a redeemed Kate and Isabel can find herself the wife of a redeemed Osmond.

After *The Wings of the Dove* certain changes appear in James's moral attitude. To begin with, the esthetic view of life—"the mere aesthetic instinct of mankind," as Densher bitterly recognized it— is presented in a much more favorable light than heretofore. Correspondingly, the Americans' moral view is much less favorably depicted; it is seen rather as a moralistic view, developing the qualities of rigidity, provincialism, and narrowness already latent in the Wentworth family of *The Europeans.* James had in fact almost embraced the moral attitude of Balzac, as he defined it in an essay published over a quarter of a century earlier:

> Balzac . . . found himself as a matter of course more in sympathy with a theory of conduct which takes account of circumstances and recognizes the merits of duplicity, than with the comparatively colourless idea that virtue is nothing if not uncompromising.[22]

The wide-eyed naïveté and childlike good-heartedness of the American hero is also given a much more severe evaluation. The lack of experience in those American lambs was always regrettable—one felt them quite unprepared for civilized adult life in a sophisticated society; but they usually had our sympathy, while those who victimized them earned our indignant censure. Yet with the exception of Daisy Miller, those heroes and heroines seemed never to be positively, actively evil in their state of unpreparedness for life. After *Wings,* however, James is ready to condemn protracted innocence as something very like positive evil. In this he follows William Blake; and after all his position is like that of any modern reader who feels quite rightly that childish naïveté is appropriate to childhood but that it is seriously wrong to prolong that condition into the years of adulthood. James continues to avoid the easy melodramatic depiction of the absolute dichotomy of good and evil; the distinction, nevertheless, is clear enough.

[22] "Honoré de Balzac," *French Poets and Novelists,* ed. Leon Edel (New York: Grosset and Dunlap, 1964), p. 87.

In 1903 James published the novel he regarded as "frankly, quite the best, 'all round,' of my production." [23] *The Ambassadors* gives no sign of threatening to stiffen into allegory but maintains its thick envelope of realism pliable and intact. The subject, James tells us in his preface, is Strether's advice to Little Bilham—"Live all you can; it's a mistake not to." The Notebooks record (October 31, 1895) the dropping of the grain: James recalls his young friend Jonathan Sturges telling of meeting William Dean Howells in Paris, come over to visit his son at the Beaux Arts and now virtually in the evening of life, and of Howells' saying "Oh you are young, you are young—be glad of it: be glad of it and *live*. Live all you can: it's a mistake not to. . . . Live!" [24] Why that suggestive grain should just then have rooted and begun to sprout is not easy to say; James was himself, however, then in his early fifties and had just come through his rather disastrous experience with the theater and returned gratefully to his own old pen of novel-writing. He may have felt acutely the urgent pertinence of the advice. But beyond that, Howells' words must have struck an echo from something still afloat in the deep well of James's consciousness—advice that he had put rather facetiously into the mouth of a fatuous young American in an early story, "A Bundle of Letters" (1879). The youth's letter to his friend, Harvard Tremont in Boston, clarions out: "The great thing is to *live*—to feel, to be conscious of one's possibilities. . . . There are times, my dear Harvard, when I feel as if I were really capable of everything—*capable de tout*, as they say here— . . . . Oh to be able to say that one has lived—*qu'on a vécu*, as they say here—that idea exercises an indefinable attraction for me." He adds that "in Boston one can't *live*," nor could he on his earlier visit in company of the Johnsons; and in describing their limitations he raises another echo for *The Ambassadors*: "With the Johnsons . . . the whole outlook or at least the whole medium—of feeling, of appreciation—was grey and cottony, I might almost say *woolly*." The name of this dazzling correspondent is Louis Leverett, which is rather like the first two-thirds of Strether's name—Lewis Lambert—which, Maria Gostrey reminds us in *The Ambassadors*, is the name of one of Balzac's novels. The final curious connection is that in "A Bundle of Letters" little Louis Leverett confesses "I've always been intensely interested

[23] *The Art of the Novel: Critical Prefaces by Henry James*, ed. R. P. Blackmur (New York and London: Charles Scribner's Sons, 1953), p. 309.
[24] *Notebooks*, p. 226.

in Balzac," [25] and spends a paragraph discussing him and some of his characters. The material used satirically in "A Bundle" becomes the matter of profound seriousness in *The Ambassadors*, twenty-odd years later, recalled by Howells' advice to James's young friend.

The Ambassadors is very much Lambert Strether's story: it is told from his point of view and our interest is directed quite as much to the point as it is to the view. He is puzzled, there is much he does not know what to make of; and we are as interested in what he does make of it as in what is actually going on. Strether is the subject. What happens in the novel matters according to the extent of its effect on Strether.

Strether is like the other heroes of James's international stories in that, despite his age, he is clearly a *naïf*. He has had some modest success in his life at home in Woollett, but is a wide-eyed lamb in the great world of Europe. Furthermore, he comes into that world not in utter nakedness but trailing clouds of New England Puritanism. The Newsome family, whose ambassador he is, would be quite at home as neighbors of the Wentworths of *The Europeans*—Mrs. Newsome, indeed, is an exaggerated female counterpart of Mr. Wentworth, *pater familias*. Yet Strether is not Waymarsh—and that is exactly one of Waymarsh's chief functions in the novel: to illustrate what Strether might have been, but is not. Strether had been to Europe briefly as a young man but, rather like poor Caroline Spencer of "Four Meetings," missed his Europe. He returns now, late, with a sense that he can make up for what he missed even while carrying out his embassy. His understandable eagerness to see the best in everything, combined with his inexperience and consequent naïveté, makes Strether liable to cruel and harmful deception—makes him as vulnerable as Jamesian heroes regularly are.

As American "ambassador" to Europe, Strether is therefore handicapped by two complementary weaknesses, and both are visual weaknesses. He suffers first from the severe restriction of vision caused by the blinkers his Woollett training—his New England conscience—has imposed on him; and this tends to give him the narrow moralistic view shared by Waymarsh, Mrs. Newsome, and all the Pococks save Mamie. Second, he suffers like Caroline Spencer and others from the great American disease—"the passion for the picturesque." Sufferers from that affliction wear, not blinkers, but rose-colored glasses; and that ocular aid permits them to accept too easily the mere es-

[25] *Tales*, IV, 439–441.

thetic view of Europe. Thus Lambert Strether, whose early frustrated glimpse of Europe has only whetted his appetite for what he missed, now grasps the opportunity for compensation. His great goodwill— a kind of middle-aged equivalent of the Jamesian heroines' moral spontaneity—buoys him up for the splendid experience of Europe; but does not qualify him as the best of ambassadors.

With those odd visual aids Strether is peculiarly liable to be deceived by what he sees in Europe. Strether himself is quite aware of that fact, but he is determined to learn, to get to see things clearly. He embodies within himself, however, the polar terms of the esthetic and the moralistic views, and is likewise sensitive to the nearly matching polarity of appearance and reality. His peculiar vulnerability and his suffering from the tension set up within him by those conflicting oppositions are shown quite dramatically in the microcosm of the European world, Gloriani's garden. Strether has seen the wonderfully improved Chad and has learned of his attachment to Madame de Vionnet and her daughter Jeanne. Bilham has called it "a virtuous attachment." [26] Now Strether is to meet the ladies, and he is full of questions. In the exchange of question and answer Strether's dilemma is sharply defined; his question points to Madame de Vionnet and Jeanne:

> "They then are the virtuous attachment?"
> "I can only tell you that it's what they pass for. But isn't that enough? [asks Bilham] What more than a vain appearance does the wisest of us know? I commend you," the young man declared with a pleasant emphasis, "the vain appearance." (XXI, 202–203)

Miss Barrace joins the conversation. Strether observes, "You've all of you here so much visual sense that you've somehow all 'run' to it. There are moments when it strikes me that you haven't any other." Miss Barrace agrees, but blames it on the "dear old light" of Paris: "in the light of Paris one sees what things resemble."

> "Everything, every one shows," Miss Barrace went on.
> "But for what they really are?" Strether asked.
> "Oh, I like your Boston 'reallys!' But sometimes—yes." (XXI, 206–207)

Chad and Marie are understandably concerned about what *view* Strether will take of them. They recognize that his goodwill, his

---

[26] *Novels and Tales*, XXI, 180; subsequent references are in the text.

rosy view, prevails, and set about taking advantage of that. Strether's eagerness to see the best in everything, to judge it all as pretty as a picture, works to their advantage and gives them their cue: they will arrange that Strether "sees" what he wants to—and what they want him to. They will be as actors following his direction—to please him, but moreso to please themselves. They will act out the virtuous attachment. The acting metaphor is James's, and its implications are extended throughout the novel (we will examine its effect more thoroughly in a later chapter). It begins, really, at the outset of Book Second when Strether is at the theater (appropriately) with Maria Gostrey and makes a tentative equation between the actors on stage—"a bad woman in a yellow frock [and] a pleasant weak good-looking young man in perpetual evening dress"—and the situation of Chad and whatever women (it *must* be a woman!) he is involved with: "Would Chad also be in perpetual evening dress? He somehow rather hoped it. . . ." (XXI, 53–54) Much later, when he has had a long look at Chad and Marie, he explains his commitment to them in terms that indicate he regards them as his vicars—they are acting *for* him:

". . . I'm making up late for what I didn't have early. . . . it's my surrender, it's my tribute, to youth. . . . Chad gives me the sense of it . . . and *she* does the same. . . . Though they're young enough, my pair, . . . The point is that they're mine. Yes, they're my youth. . . ." (XXII, 51)

Shortly thereafter Strether suffers one of his frequent flashes of bright light that penetrate his rosy lenses, as he wonders if by chance the Pococks might fail to see Chad's improvement or if by chance "he made too much of Chad's display"—if he were being taken in. He wonders further—

Was he, on this question of Chad's improvement, fantastic and away from the truth? Did he live in a false world that had grown simply to suit him, and was his present slight irritation . . . but the alarm of the vain thing menaced by the touch of the real? (XXII, 80–81)

Finally, after all the cards have been played and the truth has been exposed to Strether, Marie de Vionnet confesses to him—in terms of the same metaphor—that "we've thrust on you appearances that you've had to take in and that have therefore made your obligation.

Ugly or beautiful—it doesn't matter what we call them—you were getting on without them and that's where we're detestable." (XXII, 287)

But Strether has not been merely "wrong" in his view of things, just as little Bilham's "lie" about Chad's virtuous attachment has not been without its element of truth; and the behavior of Chad and Marie has not been *only* deception. In some important ways the attachment *has* been virtuous—at the very least it has taught Chad manners: Marie has saved Chad from being simply another Jim Pocock. Of course, in one sense Madame de Vionnet is strictly the bad woman Woollett thinks she is, involved in the "typical tale of Paris." (XXII, 271) The point is, however, that that does not completely account for her; for she is, on the other hand, quite as wonderful as people say she is. Strether's problem has been a failure to see both sides of the situation, an inability, indeed, to understand that people and situations can have more than one side. He has been taught to believe that the difference between good and evil is a matter of clear distinctions, of obvious, melodramatic, black-and-white division. He has seen the apparent good in the improved Chad and in the lady Marie and cannot conceive that there could be anything else beneath the surface: life has seemed, as the novel repeatedly suggests, as pretty as a picture. Consequently, Strether suffers a rude shock when he finally perceives, like Merton Densher, the "smudge of mortality." We can hardly miss the point, late in Book Eleventh, when Strether is enjoying his picture of the Paris suburbs—it is "a Lambinet"—until two figures in a boat float into the composition. With all the implicit evidence of the intimacy—the unvirtuous aspect—of their attachment, the intrusion of Chad and Marie applies the fateful smudge to Strether's picture. The result is to convince him, momentarily, that Woollett was right after all. But his balance returns and he sees truly what this human attachment has amounted to: it is neither black nor white but, like most human beings and their relationships, one of a variety of shades of gray. Strether can now look upon what appears and perceive the reality at the same time. With both rose-colored glasses and New England blinkers off, he sees clearly at last. Thus he is proved to have been justified in encouraging Chad, against Mrs. Newsome's wishes, to remain in Paris—not only for his own benefit, the continuing of his "improvement," but also for Marie's benefit. He is at the same time unjustified in encouraging an adulterous union.

So far as the situation of Chad and Marie is concerned, the cards are stacked: there is really no good solution to their dilemma. The fault may lie in their human weakness, or in the social arrangement whereby Marie was married, conveniently, to Monsieur de Vionnet and remains without the possibility of a dissolution of that bond. It is tempting to say that Chad ought never to have become involved with Marie; but then he would have missed the improvement brought to him by that involvement. That remains a problem, and it remains one for Strether. What is clear enough, at last, however, is that so far as Strether himself is concerned *his* problem is solved; and his experience of Europe and of Chad and Marie and of the Pococks in Europe, has at once plunged him deeply into his problem and finally brought him out. To say it again, Strether's experience has opened his eyes truly, has given him full consciousness of life. And the good of that is what the novel has to express.

James averred that the subject of his novel lies in Strether's admonition to Bilham: "Live all you can; it's a mistake not to. It doesn't so much matter what you do in particular, so long as you have had your life." (XXI, 217) What is most significant about that advice is that Little Bilham misremembers it, and the particular error in his faulty recall is what matters supremely. He reminds Strether, a little later: "Didn't you adjure me, in accents I shall never forget, to see, while I've a chance, everything I can?—and *really* to see, for it must have been that only you meant." (XXI, 278) The novel has thus made the equation, to live is to see; Bilham has been mistaken, but the novel never corrects that mistake—it develops and develops the truth that lies within it. *The Ambassadors,* then, seems to suggest that vision is its own reward. Strether gains that, he needs nothing more; to have that is to have life—and it does not so much matter what he will now do in particular so long as he has had his life.

It may be pertinent to add a word here that James had to say about consciousness in an article he wrote a few years after the publication of *The Ambassadors.* In "Is There a Life After Death" (1910), he says that as he has grown older he has experienced in his life a process

which I can only describe as the accumulation of the very treasure itself of consciousness. I won't say that "the world," as we commonly refer to it, grows more attaching, but . . . that the universe increasingly does, and that this makes us present at the enormous multiplication of our possible relations with it; relations . . . filling us . . . with the unlimited vision of being. This mere fact . . . strongly reminds one that even should one cease to be in love with

life it would be difficult, on such terms, not to be in love with living.
Living, or feeling one's exquisite curiosity about the universe fed
and fed, rewarded and rewarded . . . becomes thus the highest good
I can conceive of . . . ; all of which illustrates what I mean by
the consecrated "interest" of consciousness.[27]

That attitude is strongly implicit in all of James's fiction, and particularly so in *The Ambassadors*.

It may help us to understand the conclusion of the novel, which
has puzzled and disappointed a number of readers. Why, they ask,
does Strether refuse Maria Gostrey, who has been so good to him and
would be so good for him, and return alone to America? The answer is
simply that accepting Maria would be a superfluous gesture for
Strether: in the terms of the novel he has gained the important benefit. To demand that he marry and live happily ever after is to confess
ourselves influenced unduly by the explicit distributive justice of too
many novels—"a distribution at the last of prizes, pensions, husbands,
wives, babies, millions, appended paragraphs, and cheerful remarks"
(as James sardonically expressed in "The Art of Fiction").[28] Strether's career has been completely shaped; to wed him to Maria would
be to underline the obvious—to add an Aesopian moral to a story
already redolent with moral significance.

It is difficult, in spite of all, not to feel some regret that the situation of Chad and Marie de Vionnet is left without some fortunate
resolution; and one can even sympathize with those who are disappointed at Strether's not taking Maria Gostrey to wife. Our response
is one not only conditioned by reading novels with comfy happy
endings: it is a response to an unmistakable tendency in this and
other stories of James's, to a kind of yearning to overcome the dichot-
omies and achieve a satisfactory compromise between the opposed
items—to a desire to wed his American successfully to his European,
in a word. *The Golden Bowl* (1903) presents a happy coincidence
in that this novel, his last extended treatment of the international
theme, quite distinctly holds out to us the promise of a happy and
successful union of the American and the European.

The germ of the story James first recorded in his Notebooks in
November of 1892 as a possible subject for a short story. He returned to the idea just over two years later, considering it in close
connection with the germinal idea for *The Wings of the Dove*. There

[27] Quoted in *James Family*, p. 610.
[28] *Future of the Novel*, p. 8.

are some similarities between the two heroines, Milly Theale and Maggie Verver; but their differences are instructive. Maggie is in robust health and is something more than the potential heiress of all the ages. She is not necessarily more wealthy than Milly, but her possessions—hers and her father's—are more palpably present in the novel, and notable among them is the Prince Amerigo. For the Ververs participate, but quite without malevolence, in the practice of collecting human beings—a practice that has characterized many of James's villains in other stories. The Ververs, however, collect out of a kind of naïveté.

Maggie is indeed typically naïve and innocent. Her innocence, however, is extreme; her unselfishness is extreme: her virtues, in fact, are all exaggerated or excessive. And that excess comes to constitute a positive, active evil in the novel. Her unselfishness toward her husband, on whom she makes no demands and to whom she allows perfectly free rein, and toward her father, whom she carefully tends in order to prevent his feeling lonely and neglected, that unselfishness is as responsible as anything else in the novel for fostering the adulterous relationship of Amerigo and Charlotte Stant. James is quite Blakean in *The Golden Bowl* in insisting that childish innocence protracted into adulthood becomes positively evil. It is clear that despite her marriage to the Prince, in spite of the birth of the Principino, Maggie has remained foolishly virginal.

This is especially so in that Amerigo would make her a good husband if only she would properly accept him. With his suggestive name and his Columbian ancestry, Amerigo is obviously the ideal consort destined to the American heiress of all the ages. He is, of course, sophisticated where Maggie is naïve, experienced where she is innocent; and he lacks what he feels to be the moral fervor of the Ververs: Amerigo early confesses that he has no moral sense—only the esthetic. He is guided by his taste. But his living by the esthetic sense alone does not really make him another Gilbert Osmond (although the comparison is instructive). Amerigo's esthetic sense is like the moral spontaneity of earlier Jamesian heroines—not evil, just insufficient. And so he feels it himself.

The insufficiency of that guide to conduct appears most urgently in Amerigo's adultery with Charlotte, yet it hardly renders him damnably culpable. As Charlotte explains, during their weekend at Matcham, Maggie has virtually thrown them together by her obsessive attention to her father and consequent neglect of her husband. And it is Charlotte, after all, who is and has been from the beginning the aggressive partner in their relationship. Amerigo is rather in the position of Fielding's Tom Jones (whose philandering disturbs the morally sensitive among us): he does not seek illicit relations with ladies but is merely the accommodating gentleman—an instance of *noblesse oblige.* If we ask in indignation, "doesn't it look wrong to Amerigo?" we can be sure that his answer would be, "Ah, but it mustn't *look* wrong, least of all to dear Maggie, whom I wouldn't hurt for the world." And his answer would be, in his eyes, quite unhypocritical.

Maggie's awakening comes, as it does to all of James's heroes, with a recognition of the evil as evil; for her it is the recognition of the relationship of Amerigo and Charlotte. Fortunately, it also includes the consciousness, not that she is losing her husband, but (as the choral Fanny Assingham points out) that she has never *had* him. That recognition is beautifully expressed in the image of the pagoda in the garden, which opens the second book of the novel: it is in the Edenic garden of Maggie's protracted innocence, and it represents her union with Amerigo, but because it is in the garden it permits her no entrance. Maggie might say, with as much truth as Juliet did, "I have bought the mansion of a love and not possessed it." Her task, then, is to win her husband to her without defeating him—to redeem, not conquer. Maggie's enlarged consciousness permits her to see that she must not overcome him but simply *come to him,* to see, furthermore, that the task is hers, that it is all in her hands—the life of Amerigo and Adam and even Charlotte.

The image of the golden bowl itself helps to express that idea. It is of course a complex image suggesting at times the "love" of Amerigo and Charlotte, at times Amerigo's love for Maggie, at times her love for Adam. The purchase of the bowl has revealed to Maggie the relationship of Charlotte and Amerigo—a relationship too intimate and of too long standing to be admitted by them to Maggie. As she explains its awful significance to Fanny Assingham, Fanny decides that the simplest thing to do is to break the bowl, to get rid of the damning evidence, to sweep the dirt under the carpet. But when the golden bowl is broken, Maggie gathers it up in her hands. The gesture is eloquent, and perhaps gains from our recognizing the source from which James drew the symbol of the golden bowl—Blake's epigraph to "The Book of Thel":

> Does the Eagle know what is in the pit?
> Or wilt thou go ask the mole?

Can Wisdom be put in a silver rod,
Or Love in a golden bowl?

Maggie also sees what her task must be: she must overcome her virginal innocence and her excessive virtue—her supererogatory morality—and selfishly desire her husband, selfishly sacrifice her father and Charlotte. She must indeed descend into the arena of the world and fight her battle according to its rules—not for the world's sake but, as she repeatedly explains to Fanny, "for love." She holds herself ready to lie and to deceive—and does so, for love— always to the end of triumphing over nothing but lies and deceitfulness, and of claiming her husband. One temptation, and that a dear one, she must alertly guard against. In order to persist in her endeavor to win Amerigo to her, to make him see her love, she must not be distracted; and in Amerigo's awareness that Maggie is "suspicious" and his concern lest she demand explanations and clarifications, he resorts to his masculine power of attraction—he embraces his wife. The force of Amerigo's attraction, his physical desirability, to Maggie is made patently clear. She requires all her *moral* strength not to yield to that force until her end is accomplished. Maggie's position in this matter is very like that of Isabel Archer's at the close of *The Portrait of a Lady*, where she is faced with the impressive appeal of Caspar Goodwood's embrace—his offered love, satisfaction, and protection. If Isabel is to persist in the path she *knows* must be hers, she has to refuse the rich temptation that embrace extends. Maggie, likewise, must resist and postpone, must work for the redemption of Amerigo and the establishment of their complete love.

Early in the novel Fanny Assingham is permitted a remark that establishes a significant equation—much like the equation of living and seeing in *The Ambassadors*. She says to her husband, "Stupidity carried to a certain point is immoral; and what is morality but high intelligence?" [29] Maggie's intelligence has resulted from the shock of recognizing the evil in which she has been involved, and it becomes productive in her decision to set her house in order. With the arrangement of Adam and Charlotte to depart for America, and Maggie's first test in the farewell to Charlotte, Amerigo's intelligence is also at last awakened, his vision cleared. He becomes fully conscious of Maggie's endeavors and her worth, sees and appreciates her refusal to express recriminations, her refusal to entertain

---

[29] *Novels and Tales*, XXIII, 88; subsequent references are in the text.

explanations. His last speech to Maggie is heavy with significance, with implicit hope and promise for their future. Maggie alludes to his seeing how wonderful Charlotte has been at the last; he replies, "See? I see nothing but you!" (XXIV, 369) And with that all is said.

The moral discovery of *The Golden Bowl* is the culmination, in a sense, of the moral exploration in which all of James's international fiction has been involved up to that time. The potential of the unformed American is realized in contact and conjunction with the traditionally formed European—the moral spontaneity of the innocent American finds meaningful expression in the conventional manners of experienced Europe. The esthetic attitude is redeemed by the infusion of moral fiber; the stiffness and narrowness of the provincial moralistic attitude of the American is broadened and made more pliable by the humane influence of European culture. *The Golden Bowl* insists, like other of James's stories before it, on the importance of full consciousness, clear vision, to successful life—life in which the saving benefice of love can be enjoyed. To put it simply, *The Golden Bowl* achieves that compromise toward which all of James's stories on the international theme seem to have been striving—here the American is successfully wedded to the European, and the Principino is the pledge of the success of that union.

The stories devoted to the international theme, with their interesting realistic surfaces, are ultimately metaphoric in that James uses the terms of characterization of both American and European people, settings, and institutions in such a way as to make his expression applicable to the human condition generally. The surface lets us know certain facts of life as it was in the late nineteenth and early twentieth centuries; the metaphoric depth of the stories tells us the truth about life as it always has been and must be—the truth as James perceived it. Moral behavior, the stories tell us, involves both the appearance as well as the *reality* of goodness; and social good is that which best contributes to genial intercourse among civilized human beings. To live in the world and have any useful effect at all, one must live according to the world's terms—but one need not therefore surrender to the merely worldly. One may in fact help to redeem the world by employing its terms for nonworldly ends, not materialism, not benighted selfishness, not manipulation of others for one's own satisfaction; but for love in the broadest sense, for the realization of human potential, for the optimal functioning of civilized human society. One must depend for this not on the dictates of laws, but on the enlightened indwelling spirit of love: the fully conscious Jamesian character, like the Pauline Christian, is above the law; and convention does not dictate to him, but he makes conventional behavior faithfully express his own being.

3

FICTION II: THE DILEMMA OF THE ARTIST

IN THIS BOOK James's second great theme is called "the dilemma of the artist"—rather than "the artist life" or "the life of art" or whatever—because that is the way in which the situation of the artist presented itself to him. The idea of the dilemma and of treating it in fiction came to him early and remained. The opening paragraph of his preface to *The Tragic Muse* (appropriately) offers this account:

> What I make out from furthest back is that I must have had from still further back, must in fact practically have always had, the happy thought of some dramatic picture of the "artist-life" and of the difficult terms on which it is at the best secured and enjoyed, the general question of its having to be not altogether easily paid for. To "do something about art"—art, that is, as a human complication and a social stumbling-block—must have been for me early a good deal of a nursed intention, the conflict between art and "the world" striking me thus betimes as one of the half-dozen great primary motives.[1]

His stories of writers and artists portray the dilemma of the artist in an uncongenial world peopled principally by a public fundamentally inimical to art. It can easily be imagined that James was more intimately involved in these stories, which touched the very quick of his being. They were written, significantly, at moments of particular crisis in his own career: a large number of them cluster around the period of his experiment in the theater; and often the hero of the story is the same age as James was at the time of writing. This is not to suggest that they are autobiographical in any strict sense: if they treat of his own dilemma, the treatment is completely objectified.

Varied as they are, the stories that developed this theme can be conveniently divided into two groups. The first deals with the di-

[1] *Art of the Novel*, p. 79.

lemma of "lionization"; the second deals with the conflict between popular demand and artistic integrity. Stories of the first group depict a gross and impercipient public that romantically values the artist for the qualities that make the best show—the number or size of his productions, his personal *charisma* or *élan,* his exotic life, or whatever—and that pays little heed to what is really his most important claim to attention, his art. The world cannot—or at least it does not—distinguish between his artistic being and his mere physical person, or between his productions as artistic expression and his works as merely items in a catalogue.

"The Death of the Lion" (1894) is a typical example of the stories of this group. Neil Paraday is lionized by a society that has read about him in *The Empire* (a journal), but has read next to nothing of what he himself has written. The journalist Morrow, who comes to interview Paraday and whose article contributes to the artist's social success, is a brutal representative of the lionizing public: his failure to attend to the narrator's plea to look at the books rather than at the man is emphatically symptomatic. The sympathetic narrator's attempt to interest Morrow in Paraday's new book—"His life's here"—falls flat; so does his explanation that what an artist has to tell us is to be found in its perfection in his works, not in a personal interview. He urges plaintively and vainly that the best interviewer is the best reader.[2] As the narrator has feared, Paraday's social success virtually kills him. The brutality of the lionization is rendered dramatically poignant by the fate of his last manuscript: his best work, it is passed around callously in the social gathering like some curious artifact and finally just dropped somewhere—irretrievably lost.

The narrator and Miss Fanny Hurter are exceptions in refusing to contribute to the lionization, and in their characterization James adds a touch that recurs in the stories of artists. Fanny Hurter is spoken of as having "the face of an angel" (XV, 131); the narrator frequently expresses his admiration of Paraday in similar terms—"a big brush of wings . . . the sense of an angel's having swooped down and caught him to his bosom (XV, 105)—and Paraday's devotion to his art is called "the monastic life, the pious illumination of the missal." (XV, 124) The same figurative motif is introduced in the very title of "Broken Wings" (1900), the story of two artists, Stuart Straith and Mrs. Harvey. They are not exactly lionized, but they suffer from the pressing social demands at the

---

[2] *Novels and Tales,* XV, 119; subsequent references are in the text.

countryhouse of Mundham (aptly named to suggest one term of the opposition between art and the world, *ars et mundus*). Stuart and Mrs. Harvey are more fortunate than Paraday in that they ultimately escape the threatening pressure, but their story expresses basically the same dilemma—demands on the social person that jeopardize the artist's existence.

The Tragic Muse (1890) also affords an example of the mistaken and destructive effect of personal demands on the artist, especially in the case of Peter Sherringham and Miriam Rooth. His are the most personal and pressing: he wants Miriam for himself, by marriage if necessary, and not for the stage. (We shall consider this novel more fully later in this chapter.) The same misdirection of attention—to the personal life and away from the work produced—is a central concern of "The Real Right Thing" (1899). The point is driven home in the harrowing experience of Ashton Doyne's widow and his biographer, George Withermore: Ashton Doyne's ghost appears to warn them away from their task of writing his biography.

Finally, another of James's best stories, "The Figure in the Carpet" (1896), will serve to complete the series. It is nicely complementary to "The Death of the Lion." While in Paraday's case the focus is on the excessive attention paid to the person of the artist, in Hugh Vereker's case the focus is on the inadequacy of the attention given to his work, the failure of perception—"limp curiosity," in James's phrase.[3] The story has fascinated readers and puzzled them because they treat it like a mystery story: they are intent, like the narrator, on finding out what *the figure* actually is. Of course one must find out what that is, but most puzzled readers expect the answer to be some message or moral, some explanation. The figure, however, is none of those things: it is simply Vereker's style, the informing pattern of expression. Not the message, not the pearls of wisdom, but the *arrangement* of those pearls: " 'It's the very string,' [Vereker] said, 'that my pearls are strung on!' "[4] To miss that, of course, is to miss the *art* of his creations. To discover this "secret" demands patient, *devoted* attention. The story suggests that it is most readily discoverable by those who know what love is. Two ideal readers of Vereker's works are the affianced George Corvick and Gwendolyn Erme, who do discover the secret of the figure. And part of their proper devotion is expressed in their de-

[3] *Art of the Novel*, p. 229.
[4] *Novels and Tales*, XV, 240; subsequent references are in the text.

termination not to consult Vereker or even to see him; they will simply read his work and seek the answer there. (Fanny Hurter similarly religiously avoids Neil Paraday: she is "one of the right sort." [XV, 129]) The narrator never finds out. He wants to be told. He reaches the point, after Corvick's death, of asking himself "Was the figure in the carpet traceable or discernible only for husbands and wives—for lovers supremely united?" (XV, 265) He even entertains the idea of marrying Gwen to learn the truth! Of course he dares not. His failure is his incapacity for devotion, his misunderstanding of love.

Another note must be added here to forestall the action of that ingenuity which would claim that the figure *is* after all a message— a message about love. For there seems to be, in addition to the foregoing, a distinct "clue." When George cables Gwen to tell her he has discovered the secret, she of course believes him, although the narrator remains skeptical; the phrase she chooses to support her conviction is a line from Virgil's *Aeneid*—*Vera incessu patuit dea* (XV, 251)—which refers to Aeneas' recognition of Venus, his mother. But James elsewhere made specific his association of Venus and art. In *The Tragic Muse* Nick Dormer explains to Gabriel Nash that he must give up his political career and become an artist because of the compelling demand of art, which is not to be denied: "I'm stricken . . . '*C'est Vénus toute entière à sa proie attachée'*— putting Venus for art." [5] Furthermore, Aeneas recognizes Venus (*Vera dea*) by the *style* of her movement. The last item to notice is that Gwen Erme's second novel, published after the discovery and after George Corvick's death, strikes the narrator as a marked improvement over her first; and his grudging praise is phrased in telling terms—"As a tissue tolerably intricate it was a carpet with a figure of its own"! [6] He is unaware of what he has said: he still does not see and wants to be told. He represents half of the insentient mob that the artist faces, the half characterized by limp curiosity about art; the other half is characterized by its all too vigorous curiosity about the personal life of the artist.

The other group of stories about artists and writers deals with a mob that plagues the artist by demanding responsible performance from him in terms of dutiful productions regularly and punctually. The artist's need of patient leisure for his artistic conceptions to come to fruition finds itself in direct conflict with those im-

[5] *Novels and Tales*, VII, 182.
[6] *Novels and Tales*, XV, 267.

portunate demands that he hurry and produce something—something to justify his existence. If he is able to present his offering in sufficient regularity—publish books, paint pictures, carve statues that the public can handle and heft, visit and view—he is deemed a success in the eyes of the world. Yet if he does fulfill this duty as the world sees it, he gravely risks being unfaithful to the demands of his art, misdirecting his energies, rendering all to Caesar. The conflict, briefly, is between what the world wants him to *do*—produce —and what his art requires that he *be*—an artist.

The earliest story to develop this theme is "The Madonna of the Future" (1873). Its ambiguous appearance makes it puzzling: we sympathize with poor Theobald, the painter of the Madonna of the future (or the future painter of the Madonna), yet we wonder whether he is really a fake—or a joke. On the other hand we feel some grudging admiration for the sculptor, the creator of the animal statuettes, for even if his work is a bit naughty and certainly second-rate art, he at least gets things done and has something to show. Theobald has let a lot of time go by without producing, and we can understand Mrs. Coventry's explanation to the narrator: "At the first hint that we were tired of waiting and that we should like the show to begin he was off in a huff. 'Great work requires time, contemplation, privacy, mystery! O ye of little faith!' We answered that we didn't insist on a great work . . . that we merely asked for something to keep us from yawning." [7] And when the narrator raises the question of productivity with Theobold, he too gets a rather huffy and rhetorically inflated reply:

". . . My little studio has never been profaned by superficial feverish mercenary work. It's a temple of labor but of leisure! Art is long. If we work for ourselves, of course, we must hurry. If we work for *her* we must often pause. She can wait!" (XIII, 444)

Theobald's manner of expression, complemented by the facts that he has but the one little chalk sketch of Serafina's *santo bambino* and that the Madonna herself is already advanced into middle age, tempts us to dismiss the artist as rather ridiculous. We are then, however, pulled up short by his opposite number, the sculptor of the cats and monkeys—which illustrated "the different phases of what, in fine terms, might have been called the amorous advance

[7] *Novels and Tales*, XIII, 460; subsequent references are in the text.

and the amorous alarm" (XIII, 482)—who represents the alternative way for the artist. We are further influenced by the contrast of attitude in the two men toward Serafina: Theobald admires and adores her discreetly while his rival lustily carries her off—not even to the altar. And if our sympathies are thus directed away from the rival, they are to that extent left free to return to Theobald. Foolish and ineffectual as he undoubtedly appears, he has got hold of some truth: "Just as the truly religious soul is always at worship, the genuine artist is always in labor." (XIII, 457) Finally, of course, the story simply sets out the opposition, the alternatives, in extreme terms—busy artistic action that realizes little of the essence of art, and mere artistic *being* that is virtually never realized in action— seeming to encourage choice of neither but tacitly indicating the difficulty of possible compromise.

Superficial differences between "The Madonna of the Future" and later stories on the same general theme do not hide their fundamental similarities. One of the best of the later stories is "The Next Time" (1895), the story of Ray Limbert's constant frustration in his attempt to write successful potboilers. He does produce, but only exquisite works highly prized by his coterie of admirers; the wide world gapes and does not buy. The extent of his failure in the eyes of the purchasing world is measured by the success of his sister-in-law, Jane Highmore, who turns out three-decker novels with ease and who need make no distinction between the literary motive and the pecuniary. We are aided in estimating the worth of her "success" by such passages as this:

> Between [Jane Highmore] and Ray Limbert flourished the happiest relation, the only cloud on which was that her husband eyed him rather askance. When he was called clever this personage wanted to know what he had to "show"; it was certain he showed nothing that could compare with Jane Highmore. Mr. Highmore took his stand on accomplished work and, turning up his coat-tails, warmed his rear with a good conscience at the neat bookcase in which the generations of triplets were chronologically arranged.[8]

The trouble with Limbert is that, in James's words, he cannot "make a sow's ear out of a silk purse." [9] He cannot produce what it is not in him to produce: he can *do* only what he *is*. Thus he has

[8] *Novels and Tales,* XV, 175–176.
[9] *Notebooks,* p. 200.

nothing to show to compare in quantity or popularity with Jane Highmore's progeny.

Mr. Highmore has the same set of values as Mrs. Coventry of "The Madonna of the Future": as he wanted to know what Limbert had to "show," so she longed for Theobald's "show" to begin. And they are related by taste to George Gravener and even (temporarily) to Miss Anvoy of "The Coxon Fund" (1894). Frank Saltram is a fertile mind and a brilliant talker: he has the sacred flame in him, but the vessel is weak. The question obviously has to come up, and does: "But what is there, after all, at his age, to show?" [10] The narrator sees what there is to Saltram, sees the spark within him, the divine essence; but he reluctantly admits that "Showing Frank Saltram is often a poor business." (XV, 299) Nevertheless, Ruth Anvoy finally shares the narrator's vision, sees sufficiently what Saltram essentially is—in spite of his poor "show"—so that she is able to make her act of devotion and bestow on him the £13.000 of the Coxon Fund.

A slightly different turn is given the theme by the gently bitter irony of "The Tree of Knowledge" (1900). The sculptor Morgan Mallow does not enjoy popular success; but because of the sufficient dowry brought him in marriage, he never has to test himself in the market. Still the point is made when young Lance Mallow returns from some months of studying art in Paris; he has learned a good bit about art and has learned also that he himself has no talent— or at least insufficient talent to warrant further pursuit. He consequently recognizes what Peter Brench had known from the start —that Morgan had "everything of the sculptor but the spirit of Phidias." [11] Lance's recognition that his father's sculpture is void of artistic merit exposes the futility and fatuity of producing without the essential spark. Artistic doing without artistic being is deadly. The twist of irony is most telling in Morgan's chiding Lance for having wasted his time in Paris.

> His father, it appeared, had come down on him for having, after so long, nothing to show. . . . *The* thing, the Master complacently set forth was—for any artist, however inferior to himself—at least to "do" something. "What can you do? That's all I ask." *He* had certainly done enough, and there was no mistake about what he had to show. Lance had tears in his eyes. . . . (XVI, 187)

[10] *Novels and Tales,* XV, 299; subsequent references are in the text.
[11] *Novels and Tales,* XVI, 170; subsequent references are in the text.

In many of these stories James attempts to direct our sympathies to the faithful artist, or the person in whom the divine spark is discernible, and to those who appreciate what he is, by his use of a motif of religious imagery in association with them. We noted Fanny Hurter's "face of an angel" and the big brush of wings, as well as Neil Paraday's "monastic" life as an artist in "The Death of the Lion," and also the suggestive title of "Broken Wings." Theobald is spoken of—albeit condescendingly—as having "the heart of an angel and the virtue of a saint" (XIII, 477); and Ray Limbert's problem is that, in spite of all, his work persists in "addressing itself to the angels." (XV, 211) The characterization of Frank Saltram and of the admiring narrator depends to a considerable extent on the figurative use of temples, altars, tapers, and the kingdom of light. James regularly conceived of dedication to art as a religious commitment; Theobald early captured the sense of it in the sentence, quoted above, that associates religion and art—"Just as the truly religious soul is always at worship, the genuine artist is always in labor."

The phrase "in labor"—rather than *at* labor, which we might have expected—indicates that Theobald (and James) belonged to that tradition that thinks of artistic creation as the result of a kind of spiritual pregnancy. Thus Sir Philip Sidney's first sonnet from *Astrophel and Stella* ends—

> Thus, great with child to speak, and helpless in my throes,
> Biting my truant pen, beating myself for spite,
> "Fool," said my muse to me, "look in thy heart and write!"

The phrase also makes more apparent the particular relevance of the name of the inspirational character in *The Tragic Muse*—Gabriel Nash. *The Tragic Muse* offers the fullest development of the theme we have been considering; the dichotomy is as sharply stated here as it was in "The Madonna of the Future," and the characteristic terms of the two poles as clearly and abundantly present. Furthermore, the divine spirit that is supposed to inspire the artist, to impregnate his soul for artistic creation, is actually personified in the character of the well-named Gabriel Nash.[12]

---

[12] It has been suggested by Oscar Cargill, who rejects my explanation of the significance of Gabriel's name, that "James put together the names of two famous controversialists and wits whose quarrel was one of the most celebrated of the Elizabethan Age—Gabriel Harvey and Thomas Nash . . ." (in "Mr.

Interest in the character and career of Nick Dormer derives
largely from the tension set up between the conflicting demands of
duty and impulse—the duty he feels to accept the role of public
servant as a member of Parliament, and the impulse he feels to be
driving him into the privacy of the artist's studio to paint. His sense
of duty is impressed upon him by his family and its political tradition, by the vastly wealthy and influential Mr. Charles Carteret, and
finally by Julia Dallow, his fiancée—"the incarnation of politics," [13]
as he calls her. Hardly has Nick tasted the first fruits of success
in the dutiful line by his election to the House of Commons before
they turn to ashes in his mouth. He cannot escape the feeling that
in serving as a Member of Parliament, he is being false to himself.
Gabriel Nash enters the novel in time to encourage Nick in this
feeling—and in its complement: Nash argues that in giving up
politics and turning to art, Nick would be being true to himself,
to "the conscience that's in us—that charming conversible infinite
thing, the intensest thing we know." (VIII, 25) As Nick argues
his duty to heritage, family, friends, and Julia, Nash counters with
the question of Nick's duty to himself. When Nick demands proof
of the value of Nash's basis for argument, his philosophy or system
of life, he shows himself to be really arguing as Devil's advocate:
he wants to know what Nash has "to show for it." Nash's reply is
instructive: "having something to show's such a poor business. It's
a kind of confession of failure." (VII, 178) Nick is convinced.

Yet when Nash returns to Nick after some absence and finds
that he has been busily producing sketches and finishing paintings,
his enthusiasm is oddly dampened. Clearly Nick now has "something to show," and Nash is fearful lest it be "a confession of failure."
His attitude, after all, is not so odd at that: it is a reflection of
Nash's whole character, which is the expression of the supreme
importance of *being* and of the dubious value (by comparison) of
any specific *doing*. Indeed it is not too much to say that Nash
functions in the novel as the representative or perhaps the very

James's Aesthetic Mr. Nash," *Nineteenth-Century Fiction*, XII [December,
1957], 181). My explanation of "Gabriel" still seems valid, and to it I would
add that it seems likely that James took "Nash" from Joseph Nash, author
of *Mansions of England in the Olden Time*. In "A Small Boy and Others"
James recalls his childhood attraction to that work: "the tall entrancing folios
of Nash's lithographed Mansions of England in the Olden Time formed a store
lending itself particularly to distribution on the drawingroom carpet, with
concomitant pressure to the same surface of the small student's stomach and
relieving agitation of his backward heels." (*Autobiography*, p. 13)

[13] *Novels and Tales*, VIII, 75; subsequent references are in the text.

manifestation of the timeless essence of art. The novel insists too heavily on this aspect of Gabriel for us to miss the point; even the jocular tone does not cover the serious implications of his boast to Nick: "I shall never grow old, for I shall only *be* more and more. I daresay I'm indestructible, immortal." (VIII, 411) This remark occurs on the occasion of his reluctantly agreeing to sit for Nick for his portrait. Nick has made the request in even more jocular terms (and with implications quite as serious):

> ". . . Let me have some sort of sketch of you, as a kind of feather from the angel's wing, or a photograph of the ghost, to prove to me in the future that you were once a solid, sociable fact, that I didn't utterly fabricate you. . . ." (VIII, 408)

He interprets Nash's reluctance to sit as a kind of regret at being so brought *into* the universe from outside, to be reduced to the role of humble ingredient. And so on—the items add up to impress us with the notion that Gabriel is indeed an unusual creature, not only unworldly but somehow otherworldly, something like (as previously suggested) the temporal manifestation of an eternal essence.

Nash's function in the novel, his effect on Nick's life, has been to direct him from the first (it was he who "communicated the poison," Nick reminds him with conscious irony!) into the life of the artist and to persuade him to continue in that pursuit—in order to be faithful to the best that is in him. Nick has sacrifices to make —painful sacrifices that touch his family and provoke their pointed complaints. The family's opposition (only Biddy, understandably, is sympathetic) is based, of course, on its inability to take art and the artist's life seriously; and they prejudge Nick in familiar terms: "It isn't as if he'd do things people would like." (VIII, 230) Julia cannot understand Nick's folly in giving up the serious duty of political service. She releases him from his engagement. Nick adheres to the path that Nash has indicated to him—at least until near the end of the novel.

Nash plays a similar role in the career of Miriam Rooth, the actress: he introduces her to Mme. Carré, whose instruction really starts Miriam on the road to success in the theater. James worried over the unity of his novel, fearing that it would fall into two halves —the political case of Nick and the theatrical case of Miriam. Apart from various connections in the plot—provided by Nash and Peter Sherringham most obviously—the two cases are closely related thematically, are in fact almost parallel developments of the same theme. At first glance they seem opposed: Nick has given up a public career for the sake of his dearer private pursuits, while Miriam is nothing if not a public performer who rejects Peter's offer of private domestic life. But there the difference ends. Miriam's problem is even closer to that of other artists we have considered than is Nick's: she is caught between her apparent duty, imposed by her success with the theater-goers, to continue to give them what they like, and her urgent artistic impulse to move on to other plays, other experiments, and further artistic development. Both she and Nick suffer from the call to perform dutifully what the majority demands, a call that is severely detrimental to the private and personal desires they cherish as artists. Furthermore, Miriam suffers perhaps even more than Nick from a version of the "lionization" affliction (as we noted above): Peter would have her forsake the theater and devote herself only to him—as his wife, ultimately. Miriam is strong, perhaps stronger than Nick, and finally seems destined to have her way in the theater.

Nick's future is uncertain. The novel has seemed to encourage us to hope that he will remain true to himself and firm in his decision to live the artist's life. It seems to promise that like Ray Limbert and the others he will not know success as the world measures it, but will yet have followed the better way and known a higher success than the world understands. His returning to Julia at the close of the novel seems, however, to be a fulfillment of Nash's baleful prophecy that she would capture him in the end—and on precisely the terms on which he is with her. It has always seemed, however, that the novel metaphorically denies this by means of expressing the strange effect Nick's portraits have on their subjects: in a word, the effect of a Dormer portrait is to remove the subject from involvement in Nick's life. He paints Miriam and she marries Basil Dashwood and refuses to allow him to do another portrait of her; he paints Nash and he literally disappears from Nick's life; and on his engagement to marry Julia she suggests he paint her portrait—his answer is a surprising and definite "Never, never, never!" (VII, 283) In her refusal to be his subject a second time Miriam recognizes the effect of this mysterious law of Nick's painting: "it kills your interest in them [the subjects] and after you've finished them you don't like them any more." Their conversation concludes with Miriam's urging Nick to paint Nash or Julia Dallow—"if you wish to eradicate the last possibility of a throb." Nick frankly recognizes "the usual law" but suggests it might be reversed if he paints Mrs. Dallow. Miriam scoffs at him, "risk the daub." (VIII, 398–399) He finally does; and as the novel ends, he and Julia have not yet married.

On the other hand, James may be expressing here the nearest thing to compromise he could manage—suggesting that Nick is indeed continuing to *be* the artist yet enjoying some recognition from the usually imperceptive world, that even the "reward" of marriage and a life to be lived happily ever after may be just within his grasp. *The Tragic Muse* would then be an exception among James's stories of writers and artists—at least among those that make any claim to be at all realistic. There are two stories of artists, however, written in a fantastic vein, that do wonderfully achieve successful compromise, successful resolution of the artist's dilemma. They are a kind of wish-fulfillment exercise, perhaps an escape to the other side of the hedge—in E. M. Forster's sense of that phrase. "The Private Life" (1892) and "The Great Good Place" (1900) together solve the most pressing of the problems that plague the artist. The dramatist Clare Vawdrey manages, in spite of lionizing social demands, to enjoy the "private" of the title by means of an *alter ego:* there are two of him—one the social man and one the busy artist— capable of functioning separately and simultaneously. Lord Mellifont nicely balances Vawdrey in the story and adds a satiric comment on social personality: Lord Mellifont has no private existence at all! When left alone he ceases to exist altogether. The writer George Dane is similarly fortunate in experiencing a solution to his dilemma: he discovers "The Great Good Place," a pleasant retreat from the bustle and crush of the world. The "place" is monastic; Dane converses with a Brother; he recoups his strength and recovers his soul. When he "returns" to his study he finds that the pile of worldly business has been tidied up during his absence by the vague figure of a young guest who had been introduced just before Dane's departure for the Great Good Place. Of course it was all a dream— but the story makes its point through its amusing fantasy.

There are two other stories of artists from the same period as many of those discussed above that demand an explanatory word, partly because they are of a different sort of artist tale but partly also because they add another facet to the character of the artist as James conceives of him. James gathered most of his short stories on writers and artists into two volumes (XV and XVI) of the New York Edition; two notable exceptions are "The Liar" (1888), which went into Volume XII, and "The Real Thing" (1890), which went into Volume XVIII. These two deal in complementary ways with a point of ethics—a point of importance in James's system; they examine the question of the artist's *use* of his models, whether (by implication) and how it may differ from the general *use* of one human being by another—a principal sin in James's eyes.

Of course "The Real Thing" also addresses itself to the broad question of realism in art and the way in which the artist employs his data. But the immediate question in the story is the artist's use of Major and Mrs. Monarch, the shabby genteel couple reduced to offering themselves as models—models of ladies and gentlemen, for they are confessedly "the real thing." They turn out to be quite unsuitable, are too stiff and too exactly the real thing they are supposed to be representing: instead of being suggestive they dictate to the artist, and the sketches he makes from them are frankly monstrous. His pity for the pair does not prevent his blurting out in exasperation, "Oh my dear Major—I can't be ruined for *you!*" [14] And he turns again to his effectively suggestive models, the Cockney Miss Churm and the Italian lad Oronte. Our pity is in turn aroused for the Monarchs when they enter the studio and find their places usurped by the other models.

We have really known all along, however reluctant we may be to admit it, that the Monarchs fail as models, and for the same reason they have failed as human beings: there is no life in them—they are all mere surface. That fact is brought home to us by the series of images and figurative expressions used to characterize them—and especially Mrs. Monarch—images of painting, photography, statuary: Mrs. Monarch's smile "had the effect of a moist sponge passed over a 'sunk' piece of painting," "her tinted oval mask showed waste as an exposed surface shows friction," "She was singularly like a bad illustration," and so on. (XVIII, 308, 312) That series is associated with what appears to be a gratuitous piece of information—they had no children. They are lifeless indeed. But what happens to them on their discovering their replacements is a dramatic influx of life. Mrs. Monarch moves forward to adjust Miss Churm's hair—

> "Do you mind my just touching it?" she went on—a question which made me spring up for an instant as with the instinctive fear that she might do the young lady a harm. But she quieted me with a

[14] *Novels and Tales,* XVIII, 342; subsequent references are in the text.

glance I shall never forget—I confess I should like to have been
able to paint *that*— . . . . (XVIII, 344)

For *that* has been an unmistakable sign of life! When the Monarchs
turn away to occupy themselves instead in the menial role of servants
and attendants, the artist is overcome by the eloquence of what they
were doing. Most significantly, Mrs. Monarch "stooped to the floor
with a noble humility and picked up a dirty rag that had dropped
out of my paint-box." The artist has in a sense shown them what life
is and obliged them, unintentionally no doubt, to stoop with noble
humility so that they may rise again as humanized individuals. His
refusal to accept their mere appearance, their life as veneer alone,
has been the making of them. The artist has been selfishly faithful
to the demands of his art, willing to sacrifice whoever stands in the
way of those demands; the rightness of his faithfulness is attested to
by the good results that accrue for all—himself as artist, his sketches,
Miss Churm and Oronte, who get their jobs back, and the Monarchs,
who gain real life.

The obverse of this arrangement is presented in "The Liar" by the
case of Oliver Lyon: to put it briefly, he places selfish personal demands above the sacred demands of his art. He tries to use his
painting Colonel Capadose's portrait to manipulate Mrs. Capadose
into the position of wanting to confess her wretchedness to him,
Oliver, and so satisfy his nasty jealousy of the Colonel. He is jealous
of him for having married (and so happily!) the woman with whom
he had himself been in love some years before. The story, incidentally,
has often been misunderstood, for readers have been taken in by
Oliver Lyon's interpretation of things—the story is told from his
point of view. Capadose is simply not the dreadful liar Lyon supposes
him to be. That supposition is gratifying to the jealous Lyon, but
there is really no evidence otherwise to indicate that Colonel Capadose is anything more than a teller of tall tales for the fun of it.
After Lyon has begun to get at them, of course, both the Colonel
and Everina do lie; but he has driven them to it.

When Lyon has painted Capadose so as to expose him as "the
liar," he has abdicated his role of honest and disinterested artist.
The story carefully makes the point of Lyon's earlier integrity: in
doing the portrait of old Sir David, Lyon "sketched with a fine point
and didn't caricature." [15] In the case of Capadose he *did* caricature,

[15] *Tales*, VI, 406.

and for a particularly mean end. Thus, when Capadose knifes his own portrait it is the artist Lyon who is being symbolically slain. He has used his art, sacrificed it, for benightedly selfish *personal* satisfaction.

While this complementary pair are not typical of the Jamesian stories of writers and artists, they are nevertheless typically Jamesian. The other stories discussed above, with the novel *The Tragic Muse*, have much in common; and the two groups into which they were divided for convenience of discussion are very closely related. In the first group discussed we saw that the artist's dilemma arises from society's inability to distinguish between the essential being of the artist or the essence of his art and the mere physical appearance of the person of the artist or the surface of his art; in the second group the artist's dilemma arises from the need to distinguish clearly between what he *is* or desires to *be* and what the world wishes him to *do*. The Jamesian opposition between art and the world tends to emphasize the spiritual quality of art and the crass materialism of the world; that is the center of his theme of the dilemma of the artist.

There is, furthermore, a close association between that theme and the one discussed earlier, the international theme. Without unfair representation and undue strain we may say that as the structural tension in the artist stories results from the general opposition of art and the world, so in the international stories the structural tension results from the opposition of America and Europe. The first terms in each pair share many characteristics, as do the second. The dilemma of the innocent American derives from his confrontation, in Europe, with a world that takes its stand and bases its judgments on what shows—correct manners, conventional behavior. The particular evil of that stand is that it permits the grossest hypocrisy to flourish: what one smoothly does is not necessarily a reflection of what one truly is. The trouble with the naïve American is that he has no art or artifice to express faithfully to civilized European society what he really is. The mannerless American is like Ray Limbert—he cannot find the means to reach the ready understanding of the wide world. The American is threatened by awful possibilities for personal tragedy: must he, like Gilbert Osmond (of *The Portrait of a Lady*), cease to be what he spontaneously *is* and learn to *do* according to the ways of the world? Can he come to terms with the world without being overcome by it—avoid being ground in the very mill of the conventional? Coming to terms with the world, for the representative American, results in something similar to the artist's coming to terms with the general public: if he is not overcome by it (like Daisy Miller or the artist Neil Paraday), he learns to recognize it for what it is and to admit the sacrifices necessary if he is to remain faithful to what he knows to be of greatest value. For the most part, the American and the artist remain failures in the world's eye; yet they are, like Hawthorne's Marble Faun, better and wiser for their experience, for being tried in the fire. Successful compromise is seldom possible —although that, clearly, is what James's stories on both themes constantly tend toward: certainly Maggie Verver achieves it with Amerigo in *The Golden Bowl,* and perhaps Nick Dormer achieves it with Julia Dallow—just beyond the last page of *The Tragic Muse.*

Noting the basic similarities in these two major themes suggests a fundamental unity in the bulk of James's fiction, a consistency of moral attitude. The unity is even stricter than the foregoing discussion suggests: James's typical American hero and his artist both represent Man. It is quite likely that in James's eye the artist was not simply Man following a particular vocation, but Man at his successful best; that is to say that he believed that Man at his best *is* an artist. At least that was the attitude of his father, who wrote in *Moralism and Christianity:*

> But now obesrve that when I speak of the aesthetic man or Artist, I do not mean the man of any specific function, as the poet, painter, or musician, I mean the man of whatsoever function, who in fulfillment of it obeys his own inspiration or taste, uncontrolled either by his physical necessities or his social obligations. He alone is the Artist, whatever be his manifest vocation, whose action obeys his own internal taste or attraction, uncontrolled by necessity or duty. The action may perfectly consist both with necessity and duty . . . but these must not be its animating principles, or he sinks at once from being the Artist into the artisan.[16]

And James was to remember, late in life (he was 70), the essential advice his father gave to him and William: "What we were to do . . . was just to *be* something, something unconnected with specific

---

[16] Quoted in Frederick H. Young, *The Philosophy of Henry James, Sr.* (New York: Bookman Associates, 1951), p. 185.

doing, something free and uncommitted, something finer in short than being *that,* whatever it was, might consist of." [17] Although he may never have said as much quite flatly, James's works are an eloquent expression of that very idea.

[17] *Autobiography,* p. 268.

4

FICTION III: RELATED THEMES

I N 1886 JAMES published two novels that in many ways seem quite
different from what he had done before or would do later. They
are both concerned with movements for social reform and both give
evidence of the definite influence on James of Zola's theories of Natu-
ralistic fiction—notably of the idea of the experimental novel. They
are *The Bostonians* and *The Princess Casamassima*. Our concern,
however, will be to consider how they are related thematically to the
rest of James's major fiction; and one helpful lead is the fact that
in each of these novels there is a principal character who invites
comparison with the Jamesian artist-hero—Verena Tarrant and
Hyacinth Robinson.

The Bostonians, perhaps James's funniest novel, is a satiric treatment of New England reformers and especially of feminist movements. His initial Notebook entry for the novel indicates that he felt
the most salient and peculiar feature of American social life was "the
situation of women, the decline of the sentiment of sex, the agitation
on their behalf." [1] The satire focuses on Miss Birdseye and her nonde-
script entourage: the overbearing Mrs. Farrinder with her marital
appendage, Amariah; the chilly duty-bound Olive Chancellor; the
sardonic little doctress Mary J. Prance; and the attendant crew of
nonfemales—Matthias Pardon, the leering lugubrious Selah Tarrant,
and the momma's boy Henry Burrage. In the midst of this appears,
like a rose on a refuse heap, the bright-eyed Verena Tarrant.

Verena has the naïveté and freshness and simple good-heartedness
typical of the best of James's young American heroines, and she has
a gift—she is an inspirational speaker. When she first appears in Miss
Birdseye's gathering, she notably catches the attention of Olive
Chancellor and of Olive's cousin from the South, Basil Ransom. Olive
is visibly moved by the attractive young woman and she cannot rest
until she has taken possession of her; she can afford Verena certain
advantages lacking in the Tarrant home and help prepare her to work

---

[1] *Notebooks,* p. 47.

for the emancipation of women. It is also sufficiently clear that Olive's latent lesbianism is a strong motive in her taking over Verena. She also has the means to make it worthwhile to the Tarrants to let Verena go: Olive virtually purchases her from her family. Now they can read and study and hate men together. And Verena in her simplicity feels—most of the time—that she has a great career ahead of her.

But she has also caught the eye and begun to kindle the interest of Basil Ransom. His interest is in her *self*, not in what the reformers take to be her gift; he has no sympathy with them. Ransom, indeed, is something of a reactionary; his opinions expressed in the novel bear a marked similarity to those James expressed in some of his own nonfiction. Reactionary or not, however, Ransom is the only unmistakably male and masculine character in the book; and if his interest in Verena is selfish, it is neither benightedly nor perversely selfish. She is attractive to him not because of what she can *do,* but because of what she *is*—not as something to be made use of for some ulterior end, but as an end and entity in herself. His interest provides the dramatic tension of the book; he and Olive are the principal adversaries and Verena the prize for the victor.

As Verena progresses in her career as inspirational speaker on behalf of the women's movement, under Olive's jealous tutelage and later under the more elegant wing of the Burrages (they in turn have virtually purchased her from Olive), Ransom continues to pay her his personal attention. She continues to see him, for she is convinced it will not do to hide from the enemy—and furthermore, she reluctantly admits to herself, she rather likes seeing him. Ransom's persistence is rewarded by his finally being able to carry Verena away—and right at the peak of her career.

Readers sometimes feel that Ransom's winning Verena is an unfortunate turn of events, that it gives a tragic ending to Verena's life. Here, they feel, a promising career has been nipped in the bud; and they turn to the case of Miriam Rooth in *The Tragic Muse* as an analogous example of a career threatened by marriage. Miriam had great difficulty in resisting the temptation offered by Peter Sherringham, but she successfully withstood it and was able to continue in the theater. Furthermore, these readers argue, the very closing of the novel admits that although Verena accepts Ransom, she is weeping; and it adds flatly that faced with such a marriage Verena was bound to shed more tears. To argue that way one must have misread the novel; to rely thus on the statement of the closing sentence is to give it equal weight in the balance with all that precedes it, for all that precedes it denies that Verena is right in refusing to accept Ransom's advances.

Those disappointed readers have overlooked the pervasive satire of the adherents to the women's movement. It is these characters who are responsible for Verena's career: the futile and vacuous Miss Birdseye of stuffed pockets, empty head, and misplaced spectacles (in her misplaced spectacles was the whole moral history of Boston, we are told!), whose charity began at home and ended nowhere, who in all seriousness addressed to Ransom, as a felt opponent of the emancipation, the searching question "Do you regard us, then, simply as lovely baubles?" [2]; the hovering unsavory Selah Tarrant, who intrudes on Verena's guests (the larking young men from Harvard) to ask "Want to try a little inspiration?" (p. 132)—the vulturine Selah in his perennial waterproof, acting as pander for his daughter, avid of publicity in the newspapers (the acme of success in his opinion); and the emasculate Matthias Pardon, the newspaperman who will publish Verena's fame—a *castratus* fit to sing the praises of sycophantic success among the desecrating columns of newsprint. These are the sort upon whose acclaim the success of Verena's "career" depends. Readers who regret the termination of Verena's career have missed or simply winked at the unsavory quality of that misguided lot.

They have also been misled by Basil Ransom. They would prefer Selah or Pardon or the boy Burrage as attendants for Verena to the unmistakably male and gentlemanly Ransom. They fail to realize that, far from depriving her of a career she wants, his proposal of marriage opens to Verena the way of life she most desires: it gives her the chance truly to realize her own potential. The novel is full of indications that Verena's adherence to Olive's direction and the needs of the women's movement comes from her strong sense of duty and obligation. It is not even Verena's "New England conscience" that prompts her to be dutiful to those demands: she simply knows no other way. Ransom's attention to her slowly awakens desires and tendencies in her that she knew nothing about—except, in some cases, theoretically. She finds that she does not hate Ransom; she recognizes that his visits to her displease Olive, yet she accepts them— and most significantly the long day in New York, which she agrees

---

[2] *The Bostonians* (New York: Random House, 1956), p. 222; subsequent references are in the text.

to keep secret from her sapphic warder. In spite of our sense of the force of all her early experience with faith-healers and trance-speakers and assorted oddities, we recognize that Verena comes naturally by her quite feminine (as distinct from feminist) tendencies: her long-suffering mother is pleased at Verena's association with Olive, not because of her sympathy with the women's movement, but because she will hear something of the ways of fashion in a world more exalted than her own. Mrs. Tarrant eagerly shares her daughter's fascination with Olive's sister, Adeline Luna, who is a hyperbolic counterstatement to the sexless and unfeminine qualities of Miss Chancellor and the reformers in general. So when it finally dawns on Verena that her attraction to Basil is not to be denied, that it springs from the center of her innermost being—"the intensest thing we know"—we are able to appreciate the truth of her explanation: "It was always passion, in fact; but now the object was other. . . ." (p. 396)

Finally we must distinguish between that career that Verena gave up for love and marriage—rightly, as the novel urges us to understand—and that career to which Miriam Rooth devoutly adhered in spite of the very real attraction of Peter Sherringham's personal attention. Verena speaks in the service of interests that James heartily discredits in the novel, encouraging us to laugh at them in their muddle-headedness, to despise them in their impotence and perverseness—their virtual renunciation of their natural human integrity. Miriam is practicing a legitimate form of art. Verena's talent is meanly contributive, servile, functional in the pejorative sense: it serves other ends than itself. Miriam's art is properly autotelic, art for art's sake in the best, most literal sense. In a word, Verena's career has nothing of art in it and quite properly *ought* to be sacrificed to marriage—and in her own best interest. Miriam's career, on the other hand, most certainly must not be sacrificed to any other alliance—that is the burden of many of James's stories of artists, most specifically "The Lesson of the Master" (1888); it is, in James's eyes, the most sacred alliance of all. (Miriam of course sacrifices nothing by marrying Basil Dashwood; that marriage merely confirms her being wedded to the theater.) Verena has made the right choice. Her eyes have been opened, she has seen the folly and the evil of the world, has become conscious of her own essential needs and her own potential; in accepting marriage to Ransom she has accepted the best means of satisfying those needs and realizing that potential. If Basil is not absolutely the best choice, he is the best available in the world of *The Bostonians*. James had, in fact, come so close to writing a novel with a perfectly happy ending that he caught himself up just in time to write those closing words—"these were not the last [tears] she was destined to shed"—as though to add to the reader the assurance that this was not just another of those happily-ever-after endings.

He compensated fully for that ending, however, in the companion novel, *The Princess Casamassima,* which invites comparison with the stories of artists and those on the international theme. The hero, Hyacinth Robinson, is neither American nor strictly speaking an artist. He is a little bastard member of the English working class. He is also very nearly the most sensitive of James's heroes, none of whom, therefore, suffers more acutely and exquisitely than he. But as a skilled bookbinder Hyacinth is perhaps on the margin of the artist class; we are further encouraged to make that comparison by his involvement—like a latter-day Roderick Hudson—with the beautiful and capricious Christina Light, now the Princess Casamassima (as she became at the end of *Roderick Hudson*).

Hyacinth's dilemma does not appear to be exactly that of the Jamesian artist; how close the resemblance actually is we may determine in a moment. It derives in part from his rather strange heredity and from the way in which his various experiences appeal with peculiar urgency to the different elements in his hereditary makeup. We are never allowed to forget—as he cannot—that his mother was a common French laundress, the daughter of Hyacinthe Vivier, who fought on the barricades in Paris for social reform; and that his father *apparently* was the English aristocrat Lord Frederick (of Hyacinth's paternity we can never be absolutely sure). He lives with the patient Pinnie and works at a bindery; he is naturally thrown together with the workers and joins their movement for reform. The movement has his sympathy: he is his mother's son and the grandson of his socialist namesake, and furthermore he has a score to settle with that aristocratic world to which his father belonged. He pledges his life to the anarchist movement for social reform.

His unlikely introduction to the Princess Casamassima, however, calls forth another sympathetic response—and a vexingly contradictory one. The world-weary, disillusioned, and blasé Christina is herself involved with the anarchist movement and the mysterious Diedrich Hoffendahl, one of its leaders, and has sent for Hyacinth so that she might know a "real" worker. The effect of the introduction is dazzling for Hyacinth, and he is made aware of his eager sympathy with the way of life the Princess represents to him. He is also, apparently, his father's son; his right, or at least his readiness, to appreciate "the good life" as it is presented to him at Medley, the lovely countryhouse Christina has taken, is proven by his passing for a gentleman with the Princess' guests.

To call up the ghost of Emerson to give counsel to Hyacinth—as he apparently has given it to many other heroes of James's fiction—would not be of great help. "Trust thyself!" would wring from Hyacinth a reiteration of his anguished cry, "What self? Who am I?" His mixed parentage seems to him to offer no aid, and the very world he lives in is itself confused, its alliances inverted. Those closest to him offer no help. The Lady Aurora spends her time with the likes of Paul and Rose Muniment; the Princess Casamassima is devoted to the workers' anarchist movement. Paul Muniment was capable of ridiculing the revolutionists "for the entertainment of the revolutionized," [3] and Rosie simply dotes on Lady Aurora and her wonderful life. And his childhood friend, the vital Cockney Milly Henning, is bent on escaping (not too surprisingly!) the life and people of Lomax Place. Hyacinth's comparison of Christina and Milly is instructive in its emphasis on the confusion of roles as he bewilderedly perceives them.

> Millicent . . . seemed to answer in her proper person for creeds and communions and sacraments; she was more than devotional, she was individually almost pontifical. . . . The Princess Casamassima came back to him in comparison as a loose Bohemian, a shabby adventuress. . . . The Princess wanted to destroy society and Millicent to uphold it. (VI, 328–329)

The more Hyacinth sees of the way of life with which the Princess has been associated, however, the more he regrets having pledged his life, in a moment of fond exhilaration, to Hoffendahl and the anarchist movement. He begins to see that the movement is ill organized and, worst of all, without a constructive program: it is bent on retaliatory destruction, destruction of a way of life that had at least fostered the creation of beauty and of graceful and genial social intercourse. He realizes the human expense at which that way of life had been maintained, but he fears that a program of destruction will mean merely loss—and no really valuable compensatory gain. To the cry "Men must have bread," he would quietly reply, "Yes they must;

---

[3] *Novels and Tales*, V, 131; subsequent references are in the text.

but man does not live by bread alone." Poor Hyacinth comes at last to recognize that his deepest sympathy is with the great world of beauty and taste and gentle society, especially when it is threatened; yet he is pledged to contribute to that destruction. He has vowed to do something that he discovers is in revolt against his own being. Like the typical American hero of James's international stories, Hyacinth finds that his desire to remain faithful to himself—the self that is responsible for his success at the art of bookbinding, for his ready appreciation of the "good things" of Christina's way of life and of the high civilization of Paris—is threatened by the commitment and the behavior demanded of him by the world in which (for the most part) he finds himself—the world of Muniment and Poupin and Hoffendahl and even the capricious Christina. His dilemma is a little like that of the typical Jamesian artist, especially Ray Limbert; but his fate is much darker. He cannot betray his vow, he cannot be false to himself: he can see but a single option open to him, that of suicide. Not quite the "death of the lion," Hyacinth's is more nearly the "death of the lamb."

A problem with *The Princess Casamassima* is that while the tension seems familiarly structured, the values have got misplaced: the anarchist movement seems ideally (if not spiritually) motivated, while the established class, with which Hyacinth ultimately sympathizes, seems motivated by a materialistic desire to hang on to the goods they have. The answer to that problem lies in Hyacinth himself, who is one of the underprivileged and who has suffered—quite personally, if he is indeed Lord Frederick's illegitimate son—from all the deprivation the class system has wreaked upon the lower classes; yet he does not want destruction of the beauty that the class of aristocratic taste and manners has made possible. Hyacinth would defend the preservation of the good that resides in things—in *objets d'art, objets de vertu;* it is not the things themselves but the beauty embodied in them that he cherishes. That may seem an overly nice distinction, but it is a necessary one; and the distinction may be clarified by a quick glance at *The Spoils of Poynton* (1897).

This brilliant novella is concerned with poor Fleda Vetch's unhappy love affair with Owen Gereth—the unhappy outcome being largely the result of Fleda's hyperscrupulosity, a kind of elephantiasis of the moral sense. It offers another example of the evil effects of an excess of virtue. But it also has much to say about the proper appreciation of beautiful things. Much is made of the beauty of Poynton's furnishings and decoration, much also of the supreme im-

portance of taste—of the ability really to appreciate the fine things
that art and high craftsmanship can create. Fleda has that ability and
Mrs. Gereth recognizes it in her and cherishes her for it; in fact it
seems to qualify her as the ideal spouse for her son Owen—especially
since he is too much taken up with the hoyden Mona Brigstock, who
has no taste and appreciates nothing.

Fleda's ethical scrupulosity springs into action: she will not encourage or even permit any attention from Owen—even after he has
been emotionally awakened to her—so long as he is "promised" to
Mona. The reader shares Mrs. Gereth's exasperation at Fleda. Her
anguish is not simply that Mona married to her son will displace
her tastelessly as mistress at Poynton, but also that she will lose her
lovely things. (I oversimplify the complex feelings of Mrs. Gereth,
but do not falsify them.) Those valuable things then tend to become
objects of barter: Mona and Owen may have Poynton but with the
objets d'art removed. Of course Mona refuses, not because of the
intrinsic value of the things but of the symbolic value Mrs. Gereth
has thus imposed upon them. And so there develops the crucial distinction: increasingly the "spoils" of Poynton assume the role of a
number of items in an inventory to be valued quantitatively—
materialistically; and correspondingly less are they seen as objects
valuable in themselves as embodiments of the spirit of beauty—that
is, valued qualitatively. The distinction is sharply made when Mrs.
Gereth has left Poynton and gone to live at Ricks, taking with her
only a few choice objects from Poynton that she has now arranged
at Ricks with furnishings that had been in storage. She has invited
Fleda to visit, expecting the girl to be sympathetically impressed
with the poverty of her reduced situation. Fleda's reaction is just the
opposite—she thinks it all quite lovely, attributing the effect to Mrs.
Gereth's "infallible hand": "It's your extraordinary genius: you
make things 'compose' in spite of yourself." [4] But it is not just that;
it is something (Fleda adds) that will never appear in the inventory:
"It's a kind of fourth dimension. It's a presence, a perfume, a touch.
It's a soul, a story, a life." (X, 249) Mrs. Gereth suggests with a
touch of scorn that Fleda means there is a ghost attending, and
Fleda agrees:

> "Of course I count the ghosts, confound you! It seems to me ghosts
> count double—for what they were and for what they are. Somehow

---

[4] *Novels and Tales,* X, 249; subsequent references are in the text.

there were no ghosts at Poynton," Fleda went on. "That was the only fault." (X, 250)

The things at Ricks, in other words, have an aura about them—a presence or a ghost—that suggests they have been *personally* appreciated for what they are rather than for what they will bring on the market or how impressive a show they will make. They have been loved for the beauty of their being, their intrinsic worth. And that is the way in which Hyacinth Robinson appreciates the good things of the way of life the anarchist movement threatens to destroy.

The Princess Casamassima presents us with a familiar dilemma, one which faces us directly in our attempt to achieve a completely democratic society. But it does not offer a solution. It simply sets out in dreadful clarity the problem of life's unresolved antimonies—the demands of the flesh *versus* the demands of the spirit, the need for bread *versus* the need for something more than bread. By enlisting our sympathies with Hyacinth as he faces that problem, the novel enables us to share emotionally in the anguish of attempting to reach a viable compromise in life: it does what art can do—it makes clear sense of the problem.

5

JAMES'S ESTHETICS

J AMES'S ESTHETICS did not spring fully developed from his mind like Athena from the forehead of Zeus, but the fundamental principles of his esthetics underwent surprisingly little change during the course of his long career. If he was not born feeling that literature was a fine art whose aim was faithfully to represent life, his early experience of contemporary and recent literature soon convinced him that it must be so. From his initial critical review in 1864, on Nassau Senior's "Essays in Criticism," to his last in 1914, on "The Younger Generation" (retitled "The New Novel" in *Notes on Novelists*), James's implicit definition of fiction seems constantly to have been this: a realistic, disinterested, self-contained, artistic representation of life. His understanding of one or two of those adjectives modified during his career; and the perhaps conspicuously absent adjective "moral" was always at least tacitly present, but its role in the definition requires a special word of explanation, which will be given *passim* below.

The literary milieu in which James began his writing was largely dominated by romantic fiction and by taste that deemed immoral any book that could not be safely put into the hands of a Victorian maiden. His critical stance would then first oppose itself to the weakness of fiction then in popular vogue—just as Mark Twain would attack James Fenimore Cooper's "literary offenses" in order to define his own position. Twain's objection, of course, is to the gross unfaithfulness to factual reality that he finds everywhere in Cooper's work: "If Cooper has any real knowledge of Nature's ways of doing things, he had a most delicate art in concealing the fact. . . . If Cooper had been an observer his inventive faculty would have worked better." Like Twain, James will insist that the artist in fiction demonstrate a knowledge of Nature's ways, that he be a keen observer of life—so that his inventive faculty may work well.

Fiction must be realistic; it must be imbued with the air of reality. James picked up a phrase from *Hamlet* that seemed to him appropriate for expressing the air of reality he demanded in fiction: for as Hamlet uses the phrase to describe the lifelike appearance of the ghost of his father—"in his habit as he liv'd; Look! where he goes even now" (III, iv)—so James would use it to describe the apparent lifelikeness of the unsubstantial creatures of fiction. In his earliest review James praises the factual solidity of Walter Scott's creations: Scott sets before us "men and women . . . in their habits as they lived." [1] The phrase, with mild variation, keeps popping up on such occasions throughout James's writings to emphasize the importance of the appearance of reality. Balzac represented to James the triumph of realism: the "palpable, provable world" [2] of his fiction has no air of being contrived or *made up*. As a critic he used Balzac's achievement as a touchstone, accounting for failure in many of the contemporary novels he reviewed by measuring them against the work of the great Frenchmen. His appreciation of Dickens and George Eliot dwells on the aspect of realism in their fiction; he explains the weakness of some of Eliot's fiction as the result of her relying too much on imaginative invention and too little on her actual observation of life. This is not to say that James overlooked the value of the imagination: he was not always careful to distinguish between the inventive faculty in its acceptable mode—imagination—and that faculty in its defective, artificial, unfaithful mode—fancy; he sometimes used the terms interchangeably, but usually added a modifier like "unbridled" to indicate the fancy that was the defective force of invention, and certainly he cherished the value of the true artistic imagination. The heavy emphasis on observation, on note-taking, on faithfulness to the look of life is to be explained by the milieu in which he was writing and the nature of the literature he was interested in denouncing.

The most memorable statement of James's insistence on realistic presentation appears in his important essay of 1884, "The Art of Fiction":

> . . . the air of reality (solidity of specification) seems to me to be the supreme virtue of a novel—the merit on which all its other merits . . . helplessly and submissively depend. If it be not there, they are all as nothing, and if these be there, they owe their effect to the success with which the author has produced the illusion of life. The

---

[1] "Fiction and Sir Walter Scott," *Notes and Reviews by Henry James,* ed. Pierre de Chaignon la Rose (Cambridge, Mass.: Dunston House, 1921), p. 11.
[2] "The Lesson of Balzac," *Future of the Novel,* p. 111.

cultivation of this success, the study of this exquisite process, form to my taste, the beginning and the end of the art of the novelist.[3]

But that value is as clearly recognized, its opponent as strictly casti-gated, in James's last essay, and in all his essays between the two. In "The New Novel" he directs his scorn at the sentimental and the romantic in fiction as being "dodgy," as being an escape from the demands of real art—"just in order *not* to be close and fresh, not to be authentic, as that takes trouble, takes talent, and you can be sentimental, you can be romantic, you can be dodgy, alas, not a bit less on the footing of genius than on the footing of mediocrity or even of imbecility." [4] The good novelist, like the good painter, faith-fully renders the look of things.

That good faith will extend to the representation itself, to the integrity of the created work of fiction. This too was a consistent principle of James's critical position. Good fiction, he was fond of saying, undertakes to prove nothing but facts—and by "facts" he means the realistic items of its expression. Art prostitutes itself, James felt, when it arranges to serve some nonesthetic end as propa-ganda to plead a cause, to argue a position, to point a moral. He specifically denied the claims of well-intentioned critics who praised, for example, Turgenev's *Sportsman's Sketches* for its didactic pur-pose—for doing for the institution of Russian serfdom what Mrs. Stowe's *Uncle Tom's Cabin* had done for slavery in America. James insists that at no point do we catch Turgenev's work bent on extra-artistic aims, find no episode calculated to teach a lesson. The work points no moral, makes no direct appeal: any sense of moral con-cern results from the total impact of the work itself as a rendering of actual life. We might say that James believed in art for art's sake, except that the term has unavoidable pejorative connotations— suggesting preciousness, care for the turning of "fine phrases," the effete and decadent unconcern with real life; but he felt that art best serves life by being itself. He would in any case have been sympathetic with the modern critic's claim that art must be autotelic.

The principle of artistic integrity also embraces the self-contain-ment or self-sufficiency of the work of fiction. James directed that idea particularly at the intrusive author whose voice is clearly to be heard narrating the action, offering explanations, explicitly directing our sympathies, and in general exposing his creations as something

---

[3] *Future of the Novel*, p. 14.
[4] *Future of the Novel*, p. 264.

made up and hence unreal. The reader's sense of the controlling hand of the omniscient and omnipotent author, James contends, will destroy that illusion of life that it is the proper business of a work of fiction to create. In his early criticism James censured Trollope in particular for his frequent intrusions to talk about his story and even to suggest he might give the plot a different twist if he chose— which was to give the whole game away. And at the end of his career James is still addressing himself to the same problem of the destructive effect of the author's presence; in praising Conrad's effective use of the character of Marlowe to solve that narrative problem, he reaches this conclusion:

> We take for granted by the general law of fiction a primary author, take him so much for granted that we forget him in proportion as he works upon us, and that he works upon us most in fact by making us forget him.[5]

Quite obviously, if James had ever heard Flaubert's now famous dictum about the relation of the author to his created work (and he might well have), he would have given it his hearty endorsement: "The artist should be in his work like God in creation, invisible and omnipotent; we should feel his presence everywhere but we should nowhere see him." James would also have agreed with Flaubert's exhortation to writers to be expressive rather than discursive—to show, not state, to be dramatic rather than explanatory. Now it is true that in James's own fiction—as his impercipient readers never tire of pointing out—his narrative voice is often perfectly discernible: he "intrudes" often and boldly to speak of "our hero" and "our tale." But the question here is of the effect of those intrusions, whether the narrative voice speaks with authority—the authority of the all-knowing and all-powerful creator of the fictional world it is talking about. The effect of James's intrusions is precisely the opposite of that: they are usually an implicit denial of that authority. They are, indeed, very like those typical intrusions of Hawthorne at particularly mysterious or magical moments of his stories to call in question himself (in his narrative voice) the very wonders his tale obliges him to relate: he reminds us that the light was bad, or that the report came from untrustworthy reporters, or that the phenomenon was probably an optical illusion. "I don't expect you to believe this

---

[5] "The New Novel," *Future of the Novel*, p. 281.

either," the narrative voice implies; and if, as is the case in his best fiction, we are already caught up in the tale, we feel like retorting in exasperation, "Don't be so skeptical, of course his walking-stick turned into a snake!"—or whatever. So in James's fiction, he comments on the tale in the manner of a guide at a picture gallery who knows what there is to see but who makes no claim of power or control. James's own word on the matter is well represented in a letter to one of his young admirers, the novelist Hugh Walpole; it is a question of *The Ambassadors* (the letter is dated August 14, 1912), which James considered his best work, and he is responding to a request for explanation of the novel.

> The whole thing is of course, to intensity, a picture of relations—and among them is, though not on the first line, the relation of Strether to Chad. . . . All of it that is of my subject seems to me given— given by dramatic projection, as all the rest is given: how can you say I do anything so foul and abject as to "state"? [6]

The key phrases in that passage are, of course, "picture of relations" and "dramatic projection": they indicate the *expressive,* nondiscursive technique that James admired and sought in his own fiction.

Mention of technique brings us to the last adjective in the theoretic definition of fiction that I attributed to James. Certain implications for the meaning of "artistic" are already clear, for they follow naturally from what has gone before. If the novel is to be realistic, to be a direct representation of life, how must the writer seek to achieve that "solidity of specification" that is the *sine qua non* of the fictional art? He must take notes, James would say, and verify his impressions; the great Zola founded his monumental series of *Les Rougons-Macquart* on a mountain of notes, and the greater Balzac likewise *noted* widely and wisely in constructing his world of the *Comédie Humaine.* The less it seemed necessary, as James's career developed, to combat the irresponsibility of sentimental and romantic literature, the less James insisted on the necessity of an abundance of factual data. The time came, indeed, when he would regard that abundance as an embarrassment of riches. In his last essays on Zola and Balzac he points to the danger of a writer's being overcome by his data, of being mastered by the very facts that are to serve him. A safer guide in this matter than either Balzac or Zola, James came

[6] *Letters,* II, 245.

to feel, is Flaubert or Maupassant: it is selection of data and the economical use of factual detail that yield the best results, he realized. So in the latter half of his career he gradually restored the balance between observation and imagination that had seemed upset in his early criticism. Solidity—but not inundation—of specification is still demanded, but with the careful qualification specified in his preface to *The Ambassadors*:

> Art deals with what we see, it must first contribute full-handed that ingredient; it plucks its material, otherwise expressed, in the garden of life—which material elsewhere grown is stale and uneatable. But it has no sooner done this than it has to take account of a *process*. . . . The process, that of the expression, the literal squeezing-out, of value is another affair—with which the happy luck of mere finding has little to do.[7]

The process is the work of the imagination, the artist's "intellectual *pot-au-feu*" in which the material taken from life is simmered and *rendered*, until it has "ceased to be a thing of fact and . . . become a thing of truth." [8]

That, of course, is the message of James's short story "The Real Thing": the Monarchs are the actual fact and literally overwhelm the artist, while Miss Churm and Oronte—his regular models— suggest to him the truth he wants to seize. James was himself always careful to avoid the victimization of fact. People were always telling him anecdotes, often with the specific idea that they would do well made into a story; he would always listen attentively—until he had got enough, the sufficient suggestion, and then he would cut his informant off. And he would, in turn, appear to do the same for his reader: he would show him all he needed to dilate his imagination, and no more. He would not dot all *i*'s and cross all *t*'s but would arrange just enough detail (most carefully selected) to give "the look of things"—as he said in "The Art of Fiction"—"the look that conveys their meaning." [9]

Meaningful representation of life is the business of fiction: not, certainly, didacticism or moralizing, as we know, but a picture of life that is redolent with significance. And it is the formal control of his material that enables the writer to express—to "squeeze out" or set

[7] *Art of the Novel*, p. 312.
[8] *Art of the Novel*, pp. 230–231.
[9] *Future of the Novel*, p. 14.

forth—that significance. If the writer's representation is faithful to life, if he has seen life steadily and seen it whole, his expression will be as "moral" as he is himself; and if his artistic control is appropriate to his material his work will be *informed* with his moral attitude. In his early criticism James bridled too easily at the "moral question"; again one must keep in mind the narrowness of the moralistic attitude he was opposing—an attitude that he would claim was itself immoral in that it refused to look life squarely in the face, or the kind of "morality" that is exposed in Twain's "The Man That Corrupted Hadleyburg." In his demand for artistic freedom James easily resorted, in "The Art of Fiction" for example, to the rhetorical device of claiming that literary criticism is an esthetic not an ethical practice and that literature is extramoral. Yet even in that early and important essay he does acknowledge that the moral sense and the artistic sense are closely related at one point: "that is in the light of the very obvious truth that the deepest quality of a work of art will always be the quality of the mind of the producer." [10] He returned to address that question in almost exactly the same terms some twenty years later. In the preface to *The Portrait of a Lady* for the New York Edition he refers to the dull dispute over the moral and the immoral in fiction and asserts that "There is, I think, no more nutritive or suggestive truth in this connexion than that of the perfect dependence of the 'moral' sense of a work of art on the amount of felt life concerned in producing it." [11] It is, he adds, a matter of the kind and degree of the artist's prime sensibility.

That attitude explains James's insistence on the organic unity of the work of fiction—that it is a living thing, all one and continuous. The whole of the tale must express the informing moral attitude, otherwise it descends into didacticism, into direct appeals and preachments. All the parts must work together, mutually contributive, and not merely for their own sake as decoration or "fine writing." As early as "The Art of Fiction" James explains this idea of interdependence of parts, saying he could not conceive of "a passage of description that is not in its intention narrative, a passage of dialogue that is not in its intention descriptive, a touch of truth of any sort that does not partake of the nature of incident," and so on; and all these have the common aim of "being illustrative." [12]

We are thus closer to understanding what James intended by

[10] *Future of the Novel*, p. 26.
[11] *Art of the Novel*, p. 45.
[12] *Future of the Novel*, p. 15.

"artistic." The most important aspect, finally, of that quality is its dependence on form, and the achievement of successful formal control is the end of the peculiarly artistic endeavor of the writer. He exerts his control, to begin with, by following a strict principle of selection: realistic detail he must have, but he will choose the single revealing note that captures the essence of a character or the particular tone of a scene, or whatever, rather than rely upon an abundance of detail. He will similarly choose among possible episodes to develop, those which will be most expressive and most significant in the delineation of character and the progress of plot—according to his idea. Even judicious choice of names can contribute to the artist's control of his material. As we have seen in earlier chapters, James was, like many of his predecessors (and most notably Dickens), especially sensitive to names and put them to good use in his fiction. Sometimes they are just suitable sound effects, amusing onomatopoeia: Winkle, Undle, Gaw, Gotch, Crick, Pocock, and Wilmerding; others are more definitely suggestive—Mallett, Ulick, Dedrick and Booby Manger, Barrace, and the unforgettable Fanny Assingham; and still others are practically symbolic—virtually the whole cast and most of the place names in *The American,* Prince Amerigo and Adam Verver of *The Golden Bowl,* Gabriel Nash of *The Tragic Muse,* and so on. Symbolism generally, like carefully selected figurative language, can also be fruitfully employed as means of artistic control. Artists have always been more or less aware of these means of controlling their material and consequently the reader's response.

But James's increasing praise, as his career developed, of the virtue of formal control—of the supreme value of form—obviously goes beyond the familiar devices just mentioned. Quite clearly he is concerned with the total form of a work—"the whole shape of the thing," in Virginia Woolf's phrase—the overall control of artistic form: only from total formal control can a work be fully expressive of its inherent meaning. There is the famous passage in his preface to *The Tragic Muse* in which he condemns Tolstoi's *War and Peace,* Thackeray's *The Newcomes,* and Dumas' *Les Trois Mousquetaires* for their lack of compositional form: in its absence, he agrees, there may be life, "but what do such large loose baggy monsters, with their queer elements of the accidental and the arbitrary, artistically *mean?*" [13] And he expatiates on the same subject in a letter of avuncular advice to Hugh Walpole (in May 1912):

---

[13] *Art of the Novel,* p. 84.

> Don't let anyone persuade you . . . that strenuous selection and comparison are not the very essence of art, and that Form *is* [not] substance to that degree that there is absolutely no substance without it. Form alone *takes,* and holds and preserves, substance—saves it from the welter of helpless verbiage that we swim in as in a sea of tasteless tepid pudding, and that makes one ashamed of an art capable of such degradations. Tolstoi and D. are fluid puddings, though not tasteless. . . . There is nothing so deplorable as a work with a *leak* in its interest; and there is no such leak of interest as through commonness of form. Its opposite, the *found* (because the sought-for) form is the absolute citadel and tabernacle of interest.[14]

To achieve such masterful form as James had in mind the novelist must of course have a conception of the whole of his work—which is what Poe meant when he said the writer begins at the end; but he must also make exhaustive use of the particular devices available to him: not just symbolism but an integrated symbology, not just appropriate metaphors but extended or reiterated metaphor. When James undertook to revise his works in preparation for the New York Edition he carefully followed that principle, dropping from a story metaphoric figures that were merely adequate for the specific occasion and inserting replacements that definitely related to other figures already busily functioning; he thus created a linked network of expressive extended metaphor, actual figurative motifs. The writer must, in fact, compose his novel or tale in much the same way as a poet composes a lyric poem—employing the figurative consistently, and by echo, reiteration, and repetition achieve the *cumulative* (not simply sequential) effect that is a distinctive feature of the best lyric poetry. What that will lead to is a slightly decreased emphasis on the importance of temporal sequence and a correspondingly increased emphasis on the importance of spatial arrangement; fiction would thus approach the condition of painting.

It is slightly deceptive and unfaithful to speak of the artist's means as devices, for that suggests that they are tools or mechanisms that give shape to his material but are essentially separate from it—like poles and lines to shape a tent or a hanger inside a coat: a well-made coat has a form of its own and *keeps* its form (if it is a good coat), which is so to speak "built in." It is that sense of form that James had in mind. Yet one may still discuss the means of achieving it: the symbols and metaphors are not to be tacked on, they must

---

[14] *Letters,* II, 237–238.

rise out of—or rather *within*—the very material itself. It is in that sense that form *is* substance, as James has said. While the substance of art is "given" by life, the form is created by the artist. Questions of form are, therefore, what concern the true artist, and what ought to concern the true critic. We can thus understand what Flaubert meant when he said, in 1860, "The works of art which I like above all others are those in which *art is in excess*. In painting, I like Painting; in verses, Verse." [15] And perhaps more important, we can understand Flaubert's even more arresting expression of his desire to write "a book about nothing"—"a book dependent on nothing external, which would be held together by the strength of its style"; to which he added, by way of explanation:

> The finest works are those which contain the least matter; the closer expression comes to thought, the closer language comes to coinciding and merging with it, the finer the result. I believe that the future of Art lies in this direction.[16]

James believed so, too. His esthetic attitude not only resembles Flaubert's but was doubtless largely influenced by both Flaubert's theory and practice. The very year in which he published "the best, 'all round,' of my productions," *The Ambassadors*, James also published a substantial essay on Flaubert. The essay casts a good deal of light on James's appreciation of form and of Flaubert's understanding of it; James's remarks also, then, help illuminate this aspect of his esthetics. Flaubert, James tells us, regarded the work of art as *existing* but by its expression; style was therefore an indefeasible part of it, for on style depended absolutely its beauty, interest, and distinction. In *Madame Bovary* James found an almost perfect realization of that artistic principle:

> *Madame Bovary* has a perfection that not only stamps it, but that makes it stand almost alone. . . . The form is in *itself* as interesting, as active, as much of the essence of the subject as the idea, and yet so close is its fit and so inseparable its life that we catch it at no moment on any errand of its own. That verily is to *be* interesting—all round; that is to be genuine and whole. The work is a classic be-

---

[15] Quoted in Jean Rousset, "*Madame Bovary* or the Book about Nothing," *Flaubert: A Collection of Critical Essays,* ed. Raymond Giraud (Englewood Cliffs, N.J.: Prentice-Hall, 1964), p. 114.

[16] *The Selected Letters of Gustave Flaubert,* ed. Francis Steegmuller (New York: Vintage Books, 1957), p. 126.

cause the thing, such as it is, is ideally *done,* and because it shows that in such doing eternal beauty may dwell.[17]

If the work of fiction is *done,* if its form is successful, it has no further need of the attendant hand of its creator—who must therefore absent himself, cut the umbilical cord and let the finished work go free. And if it is indeed *done,* if it has achieved that "eternal beauty" James mentions, it cannot but be moral—or true, in John Keats's famous equation.

[17] *Future of the Novel,* pp. 138–139.

6

A NOTE ON NARRATIVE TECHNIQUE

THERE IS ONE ASPECT of James's technical artistry that merits special mention, partly because of his impressive development of it and partly because it led directly to subsequent advances in the art of modern fiction. That is his exploitation of *point of view* in his fiction. James himself used the phrase in connection with the question of how his germinal idea might best be approached—which side, which aspect, among the many possible, he would choose to illuminate and show to the reader. But he also used it in the sense in which his critics have regularly used it, to refer to the point of view, within the story, from which the story is presented, that is whose view of things (from among the *dramatis personae*) is used to "tell" the story. This is not a matter of first-person narration, it is simply the quasi-dramatic use of the attributed vision and knowledge of a given character or characters: we are shown what they might see, told what they might hear, allowed the interpretations, inferences, and explanations of which they alone might be capable.

The virtues of such a narrative technique are several, but to begin with it obviously is a means of removing narrative authority from the hands of an omniscient and omnipotent author. The author's knowledge is apparently limited to one character—that is to say, to one character in a given scene, for he may shift to the focus of another character in a subsequent scene—and his power limited to the ability to tell us only about that particular character. To heighten the illusion that it is indeed that given character's view we are getting, rather than the author's supposition of it, James often couched his narrative or descriptive passages in the very idiom of the character in question; furthermore, he sometimes gave such passages the dramatic quality of discourse, so that the reader's impression from those passages is quite like what he would get from hearing the direct conversation of the character. Skillful use of point of view, then, helps give the work of fiction an air of independence, helps make it dramatically expressive.

Point of view also serves as a means of focusing the action of a story, of directing attention to important aspects of the action, to the most pertinent details of description, and so on, thus lending tacit emphasis to the significant features of a story; it is, then, a means of defining the action and consequently of limiting and controlling the *area* and even the nature of the reader's responses. The reader's responses will have been awakened, James felt, through the interest that arises from the characters' concern with the meaning of what is going on: the reader is involved sympathetically by the interpreting actors.

> . . . the figures in any picture, the agents in any drama, are interesting only in proportion as they feel their respective situations; since the consciousness, on their part, of the complication exhibited forms for us their link of connexion with it.[1]

As James's adroitness in the use of point of view increased, he tended to direct the "interest" more and more onto the focusing character himself—who became less a kind of chorus to comment on the action, and more a character important *because* of his ability to speculate and comment. Ultimately, development of this narrative technique would lead to the writing of stories in which the hero would be his own historian—which sounds like no novelty—but in a new way: what would "happen" in such stories, that is, what would *matter,* would be less and less the action in which the hero is involved and increasingly what he *thought about* that action—what it meant to him, what difference it made to him, and what difference it made *in* him.

Now it might seem that the ideal story would be precisely a first-person narration, with not only the point of view but the very voice of the hero recounting the action. And so it might be, but not for the novel, James thought: "the first person, in a long piece, is a form foredoomed to looseness." [2] He felt that the author could exert less control, or exert control less effectively, through first-person than through third-person narrative using carefully restricted point of view. Although he did commit himself to one experiment of the kind in *The Sacred Fount,* it was exceptional, and his most successful novels, technically, use the third person.

The last word on the virtue of this technique for James must be

[1] *Art of the Novel,* p. 62.
[2] *Art of the Novel,* p. 320.

the assertion of its singular appropriateness for the moral attitude he had to express. We have noted that James's fiction has regularly insisted on the importance of a lively consciousness, of clear vision. His technique of point of view is then an eminently appropriate means of expressing the degree of clarity that a character's vision has attained: what—and how much—he tells us he is conscious of lets us know how good that consciousness is. But the risks for the author in such an undertaking are great, the difficulties of composition enormous—if he is committed to the dramatic method of exclusively "showing" and never telling. It seems likely that the reason James cited *The Ambassadors* as being his best is that in that novel he had pushed his technique of point of view to the ultimate—so far as he conceived of its possibilities—and had used it with complete appropriateness for the treatment and expression of his material. The achievement of *The Ambassadors*, however, was possible only after a career of experiment and variety of attempts.

When James returned to the novel after his theatrical experiment of the early nineties, he produced two novels that are especially important for their experiments in the technique of narrative focus, *What Maisie Knew* (1897) and *The Awkward Age* (1899). The earlier of these relies heavily on the point of view of little Maisie in order to relate the sordid pairings and the consequent shuffling about of Maisie that follow from her parents' separation and divorce. While James's comments in his Notebooks suggest that he wished to give a freshness of interest to the somewhat stale material by presenting it through the eyes of a little girl, the finished novel shows that James has concentrated most of the interest in Maisie—the immoral minuet in which the adult characters are involved matters only insofar as Maisie's concern with it all enables us to understand her—her imposed precocious sophistication and naïve puzzlement. What matters in the story is what happens to Maisie's mind.

The Awkward Age is an interesting attempt to illuminate the central issue of the novel through a series of reflective scenes: each book in the novel bears the name of a character whose view of the central concern is dominant in that book. Finally Nanda Brookenham herself, the central figure of our concern, is given the reflective role. No character—not even Nanda—is allowed to give complete illumination: the sum of the reflections is necessary for that. James's words on the technique of this novel, given in his preface, are unusually explicit; his preparatory sketch of the novel, he tells us, was a neat circle "consisting of a number of small rounds disposed at equal distance about a central object"—the small rounds to function as lamps to illuminate the central object, the subject of the novel. Each of these lamps was to be a social occasion, to bring out to the full "the latent colour of the scene in question and cause it to illustrate, to the last drop, its bearing on my theme." It would all be as objectively presented as a play on the stage; the actors in the novel carry the burden of presentation in their dialogue—there was to be no "going behind," as James called it, to compass explanations: the narrative voice telling us the thoughts and opinions of the actors is virtually inaudible. The avowed aim, as realized, was "To make the presented occasion tell all its story itself, remain shut up in its own presence." [3]

The technical method of *The Awkward Age* had been adumbrated twenty years earlier in the short story "A Bundle of Letters." There the central issue is life at the *pension* of Mme. de Maisonrouge in Paris; and the issue is illuminated by the commentaries in the letters of the half dozen pensionnaires who correspond with the folks back home. The principal difference is, obviously, that the short story is told by a series of first-person narrators, while the novel depends on the dramatic exposition of the constant dialogue; furthermore, the first-person narrators illuminate themselves far more than they do the central situation. Because the reader has access to all the correspondence (*from* the *pension*) and can therefore more easily read between the lines of any given letter, he realizes the extent to which the narrators are unreliable—not that they intend to be outright deceptive, but that they want to put things in the best light. We know full well as we read the conversations of *The Awkward Age* that the members of the Brookenham *salon* are deceivers, that they speak out of both sides of their mouth; but we know also that they all realize the extent to which deception is practiced and that while they may never quite know the "truth," they do make the appropriate allowances. The same cannot be said with assurance of those to whom the letters in "A Bundle" are dispatched.

While the general technical form of "A Bundle of Letters" anticipates that of *The Awkward Age*, the particular treatment of the individual correspondents anticipates somewhat the general technique of *What Maisie Knew*, and indeed a series of stories on the main line of technical development leading to *The Ambassadors*. That technique relies on the understanding that to use the point of view of a

---

[3] *Art of the Novel*, pp. 110–111.

given character to focus the action for the reader is to heighten the story's interest, but also that the interest may easily—and desirably —shift from the action of the story (as that is traditionally understood) to the focus-character's appreciation and comprehension of the action. Thus a device that is at first reflective becomes reflexive: the focus-character's view initially appears to illuminate the central issue, but gradually is understood to illuminate, reflexively, the viewer himself. We have always known that a witness's report may tell us more about the witness than about the event he is reporting; but to make that phenomenon of central importance in fictional narrative was one of James's great artistic achievements.

The peculiar difficulty in that undertaking is that it must take into account and combat the traditional tendency of the average reader to accept the authority of the reporting character—except where his untrustworthiness is clearly underlined by fictional dramatic irony. A case in point is "The Liar," in which Oliver Lyon is the principal authority, as the story is told largely from his point of view. That story has been misunderstood simply because Lyon's authority has been accepted as reliable (as explained above, in Chapter 3): he thinks, and tells us, that Capadose is a monstrous liar and that his wife must therefore be wretchedly unhappy. There is no blatantly obvious evidence to the contrary; attended to carefully, however, the story reveals in a multitude of subtle touches that Lyon is untrustworthy because his view is warped by jealousy. So as he reflects the situation of the Capadoses the real interest comes from the reflexive characterization of himself: the interest is in Lyon's warped little mind.

James was to do something similar in "The Solution" (1889). The narrator and authority in this story of a practical joke that backfires is simply wrong about the meaning and indeed the true state of relationships—most painfully, that between him and his fiancée Mrs. Rushbrook: she marries "poor" Henry Wilmerding, on whom the narrator had played his practical joke. Not a terribly successful story, its ending is too close to the O. Henry surprise reversal situation; "The Solution" is nevertheless interesting as an experiment in the development of the unreliable and deceived authority.

Two stories of 1898 developed the technique a good deal further. "In the Cage" quite clearly demonstrates the shift of the important interest from the central action reflected by the focus-character to the character herself. The unnamed character whose point of view dominates the story, a poor young woman employed in the cage of the telegraph and postal office in Cocker's store, lives a delightful vicarious existence in the world of Lady Bradeen and Captain Everard—through the medium of their telegrams. The wonderful moment arrives in which she enters that world, briefly, to add her adjustment to the lives of her vicars. It is not the action of Lady Bradeen and the Captain that matters, to repeat, but the cage-girl's perception of that action; in other words, not the objective reality of *their* world, but the psychological reality of the girl's world that provides the interest.

Most famous of all the stories in this line is the fascinating novella *The Turn of the Screw* (1898), the story of the sheltered young woman who becomes governess to the children Miles and Flora, and discovers that they are haunted by the ghosts of the departed servants Peter Quint and Miss Jessel. The story was long regarded as a puzzle: if the ghosts are *real,* then the governess is a tragic figure who struggled bravely against them to protect the children, but lost; if the ghosts are just her hallucinations, then she is a sick girl whose meddling in the life of the children is quite unfortunate and finally destructive. To prove the existence of the ghosts is impossible: the governess is the authority for all the critical "facts" in the case. It does seem clear, however, that Quint and Miss Jessel were morally dubious characters when alive and that little Miles and Flora were to some extent corrupted by association with them—precisely how and to what extent we have no way of knowing, but are encouraged to imagine the worst or at least left free to do so. Some vestiges of that taint apparently remain in Miles and Flora; in that sense at least, then, the spirit of Quint and Jessel is still with them (as we might easily say, speaking figuratively). The governess detects the taint, partly because it is there to be detected and partly because she is so constituted as to be particularly sensitive to such a taint as that. She has lived a very sheltered life, has fed on romantic literature, and recently had her own romantic tendencies freshly kindled by her introduction to the handsome guardian of the children. When she begins her inquiry into the mystery of the children's lives—as a sickly curious seeker after the unsavory and titillating associations they must have had and may still be having with the spirits of Quint and Miss Jessel—her motives are mixed: fascination with potential evil and yet an apparently quite earnest desire to preserve the innocence (or what remains of it) of the two lovely children. It will not do to say of her that she is mistaken, that the ghost business is "all in her head," for that of course is precisely the point: it *is* in her head, and that is the source of interest. The ghosts may indeed be there, at least in the rather figurative sense suggested above; and when little Flora at the shore of the pond puts one stick appropriately into the hole of another she may be guilty of an act with sexual overtones done for the benefit of the onlooking ghost of Miss Jessel, or she may just be making a simple boat. The act itself is a fact; the point is that the governess sees the act and focuses on those particular details. It is the interest of *that* psychological reality—the anxious mind of the romantic and zealous governess—that properly provides the interest. We regret, finally, that her dilemma drives little Flora away and virtually kills Miles, but we stare in fascinated horror at the governess herself: it is *her* dilemma.

The Sacred Fount (1901) has proved most puzzling of all, and perhaps the reason is that James here used the first-person narrative technique. In attempting to find out the truth of what is going on between couples during the weekend at Newmarch, the reader is at even greater difficulty than he was with *The Turn of the Screw* because the first-person narrator is quite exclusively the single authority; other characters both support and contradict his theories about various kinds of vampirism to explain the changes, both physical and intellectual, he detects (or thinks he detects) among the guests. Once again, the only hope for the reader is to let himself be entertained by the fascinating mental gymnastics of the narrator: that psychological phenomenon is the principal *truth* with which the story is concerned.

Finally, *The Ambassadors* has made full-scale and pervasive use of this technique. The story is told from Lambert Strether's point of view; he is the agent who focuses the "action" of the novel. We have seen that in some degree Strether descends from Louis Leverett of "A Bundle of Letters": that connection is as important technically as it is thematically, for the authority of Strether in *The Ambassadors* is as reliable as that of Leverett in the early short story—but it is much more subtly handled.

Strether has been sent as Mrs. Newsome's ambassador to Paris to discover the reason for Chad's lingering abroad instead of dutifully returning to the family business in Woollett. Strether focuses on and heightens the interest of Chad's situation in Paris, with Madame de Vionnet and her daughter, with little Bilham, and with all the glittering world of Gloriani's garden. Before long it is quite apparent that

Strether is not seeing what is really there under his nose; we know long before he discovers it, near the close of the book, just what is going on between Chad and Marie. But we have become interested in Strether's attempt to discover what is going on, to understand what is *really* there—to see things clearly—and thus we feel, quite properly, that Strether's view of things is what is important: what he makes of what he sees, and finally what *that* makes of him. Those are the ultimate concerns.

The matter of the story is indeed Strether's vision. The narrative technique develops that matter and shapes it significantly in a very subtle but very persistent way. The technique works—always via Strether's focusing point of view—to a considerable extent by a process that blurs the distinction between the figurative and the literal. There are two recurrent figurative motifs in the story, extended development of the saying "all the world's a stage" and of the tired simile "as pretty as a picture." They are reiterated, of course, in Strether's idiom. From the outset they are presented as figurative utterances; but the simile shifts into metaphor, and the metaphoric becomes—or is too close to actually becoming—the literal. The reverse is also true: literal details on a few important occasions assume significant figurative value. The purpose of all this is to express for the reader—not so that he immediately *notices* it (*ars est celare artem*), but so that his sensibility gradually feels the impress of it—the quality of Strether's vision: it is faulty and untrustworthy, and his authority is unreliable.

By his own explicit confession, Lambert Strether is a man of great good will; he is especially glad of his embassy because it gives him a second chance to experience Europe, after his first of many years ago was abruptly frustrated. He will do his duty but he will have his experience. He will see the best there is to see, and he will see what there is to see in the best possible light. Once on the spot he recognizes the additional boon that although he is a bit too old to live fully the experience he should have had, he can live it vicariously through Chad and his charming friends.

Now, the initial exposition given, Book Second opens with Strether and Maria Gostrey at dinner before going off to the theater. He is delighted with himself and his setting:

> Miss Gostrey had dined with him at his hotel, face to face over a small table on which the lighted candles had *rose-coloured shades;* and the *rose-coloured shades* and the small table and the soft fra-

grance—had anything to his mere sense ever been so soft?—were so many touches in he scarce knew what *high picture*.[4]

The underlined phrases indicate the specific working of the technique in question. We have no possible reason to doubt that the candles really had rose-colored shades—especially since the reference is repeated, and in close sequence—but the effectiveness of that detail is that it tucks itself unobtrusively into our consciousness of the scene and gradually impresses us with the fact that Strether's view of things has *really* had a rose-colored cast to it, as though (to state it baldly) he were looking at the world through rose-colored glasses. Furthermore, Strether conceives of this particular setting as a "high picture"—that is how nice it seemed to him. But the impression is stressed, less delicately, a paragraph later, when Lambert and Maria have gone to the theater. His delight has only increased as the rosy view of dinner persists: "It was an evening, it was a world of types, and this was a connexion above all in which the figures and faces in the stalls were interchangeable with those on the stage." (XXI, 53) And Strether recognized on stage "what he was pleased to take for the very flush of English life. He had distracted drops in which he couldn't have said if it were actors or auditors who were most true." (XXI, 53) Then the wayward Chad makes his entrance—looking immensely improved.

As the novel progresses and the plot, for Strether, thickens, these two figurative motifs recur: life in Paris seems to Strether a "square bright picture" (XXI, 164), or some variation of that throughout most of his time there; young Jeanne de Vionnet is "a faint pastel in an oval frame" (XXI, 259), and so on; less frequently but no less persistently Strether thinks of life in Paris as a drama, of Mme. de Vionnet as being "like Cleopatra in the play, indeed various and multifold" (XXI, 271), and of her introduction to the Pococks as giving "the drama a quicker pace than he felt it yet" (XXII, 90), and so on. These figurative motifs reflect the actual situation as Strether is faced with it: Chad and Marie know all too well Strether's mission, but when they recognize his good will and his ability to be favorably impressed with the fine appearance of things, they undertake to present him with the finest appearance they can show. They take care to appear to him "as pretty as a picture" and to *act out* for him what they realize he wants to see. Thus, what Strether sees

---

[4] *Novels and Tales,* XXI, 50; subsequent references are in the text.

is *really* a high picture, really a drama in which actors and audience could be interchanged. What he does not see for some time, however, is that he is looking at life represented rather than truly lived.

That recognition occurs, of course, late in Book Eleventh. And in order that we may *feel* the full significance of the revelation, Strether is allowed to set it up through the medium of his two figurative motifs—here brought together and intertwined. Book Eleventh is a whole fabric of theater and picture imagery; his visit to the Parisian suburb has been an entry into a Lambinet painting: "He really continued in the picture . . . had meanwhile not once overstepped the oblong gilt frame . . . he had never yet so struck himself as engaged with others and in midstream of his drama." (XXII, 251–253) Thus there is awakened in the reader a thronging chorus of echoes from all the earlier impressions made by the earlier appearances of these two motifs—impressions of which he was hardly aware; and the striking effect of this process of accumulation (for all the world like the effect of a lyric poem) now makes itself significantly felt and recognized.

> For this had been all day at bottom the spell of the picture—that it was essentially more than anything else a scene and a stage, that the very air of the play was in the rustle of the willows and the tone of the sky. The play and the characters had, without his knowing it till now, peopled all his space for him, and it seemed somehow quite happy that they should offer themselves, in the conditions so supplied, with a kind of inevitability. (XXII, 253)

Into this idyllic scene come Chad and Marie, in a boat, full of unmistakable evidence of the absolute intimacy of their relationship: the smudge of mortality across Strether's picture! He *sees* at last, recognizes "the quantity of make-believe" involved in the beautiful life he had been admiring, and is struck with the "pity of its being so much like lying." (XXII, 265–266)

That of course is not quite the end. Strether has also learned that the Woollett system of judging only by the letter of the law is as unsatisfactory as the Parisian system of judging only by the "vain appearance." He has learned that the evil of adultery lies not in its being condemned in the decalogue, but in its liability to consist of the inhuman *use* of one individual human being by another. Of that, and more, he has at last become conscious; and to have *seen*—as the novel clearly implies—is to have *lived*. The point to be noted is that the formal structure of the novel, largely the use of Strether's point of view as the defining narrative technique, is not only a singularly appropriate medium for the expression of the novel's matter but is virtually indistinguishable from that matter: Strether's view of things is *both* subject and technique.

The Ambassadors managed to achieve successfully the end toward which James's technical experiments had constantly tended; it represents a fully dramatic expression of its ideas, all is shown; and the technique of expression (Strether's point of view and the figurative motifs employed as an essential feature of that point of view) is the very subject of the novel itself. The words of praise James had for Flaubert's *Madame Bovary* are, then, perfectly applicable to *The Ambassadors*: "The form is in *itself* as interesting, as active, as much of the essence of the subject as the idea. . . ."

There is an additional reason for dwelling on James's achievement in *The Ambassadors*: it represents a very important contribution to the development of the modern "psychological" novel. *The Ambassadors* is the story of Strether's consciousness, caught at a crucial moment of awakening; technically it is a dramatization of that consciousness. From such dramatic exposition of a character's psychological development arose the stream-of-consciousness technique of narration, and the novels of psychological realism that stand out so prominently in the fiction of the twentieth century: James Joyce's *Ulysses*, Virginia Woolf's *Mrs. Dalloway*, Ford Madox Ford's *The Good Soldier*, William Faulkner's *The Sound and the Fury*, to mention a few of the novels in English. We can hardly disagree with James's estimate of *The Ambassadors*: it is indeed "quite the best."

CONCLUSION

THE DEVELOPMENT of prose fiction in the English language seems to have been vast and extensive in the past century. From Nathaniel Hawthorne to William Faulkner (to consider only American artists in fiction) seems a great span in the relatively short history of the novel. It is indeed striking that the fiction of Henry James covers that span almost exactly, that his career embraces that vast and extensive development in fiction during the past hundred years or so. He took up the novel where Hawthorne had left it; and when at last he set down his own old pen, James had reached that point at which the great writers of more recent years—Proust, Joyce, and Faulkner —would begin their practice in the art of fiction.

James's insistence on treating fiction as a fine art and his extensive experiment in narrative technique were of paramount importance in the development of the modern novel and particularly in the development of that form from realism through impressionism to the stream-of-consciousness technique of the giants of twentieth-century fiction. As his talent turned, toward the end of his career, to creating an almost poetic novel, in which the importance of spatial arrangement was increasingly recognized, he anticipated the artistic discoveries of Virginia Woolf, Ford Madox Ford, and his compatriot Faulkner. And the impressive quantity as well as the quality of James's achievement in the art of fiction argue for him a very high place indeed in the ranks of great writers.

As complement to his fiction there is also his important achievement in literary criticism. His critical writings, and not least the series of prefaces written for the New York Edition, are admirable examples of the art of criticism. They were in large part responsible for the development of the New Critical movement—a grateful rejuvenating and revitalizing force of recent years—offering precept as well as example to almost two generations of critics, and their pupils, and enabling the enlightened reader, furthermore, to appreciate more intelligently the art of fiction as it has flourished in the twentieth century.

His journeyman work as a practical critic helped establish many young writers, his contemporaries, whom we now recognize as major figures in the field of prose fiction. He also pricked the bubble reputation of many minor and inept laborers in the field whose appeal was to uninformed taste, to limp curiosity, to misguided expectations.

Beyond that he helped to educate his contemporaries, both through his delightful and informed travel essays and his acute criticism of art and architecture, to the pleasures and beauty of the old civilization of Europe. Much of that writing can still be read with certain profit by the young American transatlantic voyager—the passionate pilgrim of the present day.

And finally, James's artistic treatment of the material that still forms much of our own experience as modern Americans has enabled us to understand ourselves and our world more fully than we otherwise should. The least didactic of writers, James has left us a world of prose fiction that affords an important education of our sensibilities —the creation of an "intelligent heart"—without which there is little hope for a humane civilized world.

SELECTED BIBLIOGRAPHY

PRINCIPAL COLLECTIONS OF JAMES'S FICTION

The Novels and Tales of Henry James (the "New York Edition"). New York: Charles Scribner's Sons, 1907–1909 (24 vols.). London: Macmillan & Co., 1908–1909 (24 vols., 2 vols. added in 1918). Reprinted, 1962–1965.

The Novels and Stories of Henry James: New and Complete Edition, ed. Percy Lubbock. London: Macmillan & Co., 1921–1923 (35 vols.).

The Complete Tales of Henry James, ed. Leon Edel. London: Rupert Hart-Davis, 1961–1964 (12 vols.). Philadelphia: J. B. Lippincott Company, 1962–1965 (12 vols.).

PRINCIPAL COLLECTIONS OF JAMES'S CRITICISM

French Poets and Novelists. London: Macmillan & Co., 1878.

Partial Portraits. London and New York: Macmillan & Co., 1888.

Picture and Text. New York: Harper & Row, Publishers, 1893.

The Question of Our Speech. The Lesson of Balzac: Two Lectures. Boston and New York: Houghton Mifflin Company, 1905.

Views and Reviews, ed. Le Roy Phillips. Boston: The Ball Publishing Co., 1908.

Notes on Novelists with Some Other Notes. London: J. M. Dent & Sons, 1914. New York: Charles Scribner's Sons, 1914.

The Art of the Novel: Critical Prefaces by Henry James, ed. R. P. Blackmur. New York: Charles Scribner's Sons, 1934.

PRINCIPAL COLLECTIONS OF JAMES'S TRAVEL LITERATURE

Transatlantic Sketches. Boston: James R. Osgood and Co., 1875.

Portraits of Places. London: Macmillan & Co., 1883. Boston: James R. Osgood and Co., 1884.

A Little Tour in France. Boston: James R. Osgood and Co., 1885. London: William Heinemann, Ltd., 1900.

Essays in London and Elsewhere. London: James R. Osgood, McIlvaine and Co., 1893.

The American Scene. London: Chapman & Hall, Ltd., 1907. New York and London: Harper & Row, Publishers, 1907.

Italian Hours. London: William Heinemann, Ltd., 1909. Boston and New York: Houghton Mifflin Company, 1909.

DRAMA

The Complete Plays of Henry James, ed. Leon Edel. Philadelphia and New York: J. B. Lippincott Company, 1949.

CRITICAL BIOGRAPHY

Hawthorne. London: Macmillan & Co., 1879. New York: Harper & Row, Publishers, 1880.
William Wetmore Story and His Friends. Edinburgh and London: William Blackwood & Sons, Ltd., 1903. Boston: Houghton Mifflin Company, 1903.

AUTOBIOGRAPHY

A Small Boy and Others. New York: Charles Scribner's Sons, 1913. London: Macmillan & Co., 1913.
Notes of a Son and Brother. New York: Charles Scribner's Sons, 1914. London: Macmillan & Co., 1914.
The Middle Years. London: William Collins Sons & Co., 1917. New York: Charles Scribner's Sons, 1917.
Henry James: Autobiography, ed. F. W. Dupee. New York: Criterion Books, Inc., 1956. (A collection of the three preceding volumes.)

MISCELLANEOUS

Within the Rim and Other Essays. London: William Collins Sons & Co., 1919. (James's writing on World War I.)
The Notebooks of Henry James, ed. F. O. Matthiessen and Kenneth B. Murdock. New York: Oxford University Press, 1947.

PRINCIPAL COLLECTIONS OF JAMES'S LETTERS

The Letters of Henry James, ed. Percy Lubbock. 2 vols. London: Macmillan & Co., 1920. New York: Charles Scribner's Sons, 1920.
Henry James: Letters to A. C. Benson and Auguste Monod, ed. E. F. Benson. London: Elkin Mathews and Marrot, 1930. New York: Charles Scribner's Sons, 1930.
Theatre and Friendship: Some Henry James Letters with a Commentary by Elizabeth Robins. London: Jonathan Cape, Ltd., 1932. New York: G. P. Putnam's Sons, 1932.
The James Family, ed. F. O. Matthiessen. New York: Alfred A. Knopf, 1947.

Harlow, Virginia. *Thomas Sergeant Perry: A Biography and Letters to Perry from William, Henry, and Garth Wilkinson James*. Durham, N.C.: Duke University Press, 1950.

Selected Letters of Henry James, ed. Leon Edel. New York: Farrar, Straus & Giroux, Inc., 1955.

Edel, Leon, and Lyall H. Powers. "Henry James and the *Bazar* Letters," *Bulletin of the New York Public Library*, LXII (February, 1958), 75–103.

Monteiro, George. *Henry James and John Hay: The Record of a Friendship*. Providence, R.I.: Brown University Press, 1965.

BIBLIOGRAPHIES

Edel, Leon, and Dan H. Laurence. *A Bibliography of Henry James*. London: Rupert Hart-Davis, 1957; revised 1961.

Foley, Richard N. *Criticism in American Periodicals of the Works of Henry James from 1866 to 1916*. Washington, D.C.: Catholic University of America Press, 1944.

Modern Fiction Studies, III (Spring, 1957), 73–96. Revised, XII (Spring, 1966), 117–177.

Phillips, Le Roy. *A Bibliography of the Writings of Henry James*. New York: Coward-McCann, 1930.

Spiller, Robert E. "Henry James." *Eight American Authors: A Review of Research and Criticism*, ed. Floyd Stovall (New York: Modern Language Association of America, 1956), pp. 367–418.

BIOGRAPHIES

Bosanquet, Theodora. *Henry James at Work*. London: Hogarth Press, Ltd., 1924.

Burr, Anna Robeson, ed. *Alice James: Her Brothers—Her Journal*. New York: Dodd, Mead & Company, 1934.

Dupee, F. W. *Henry James*. New York: William Sloane Associates, Inc., 1951. Revised, Garden City, N.Y.: Doubleday & Company, Inc. (Anchor Books) 1956.

Edel, Leon. *Les Années Dramatiques*. Paris: Jouve et Cie., 1931. See "Introduction," *The Complete Plays of Henry James*. Philadelphia: J. B. Lippincott Company, 1949.

————. *Henry James: The Untried Years, 1843–1870*. Philadelphia: J. B. Lippincott Company, 1953.

————. *Henry James: The Conquest of London, 1870–1881*. Philadelphia: J. B. Lippincott Company, 1962.

————. *Henry James: The Middle Years, 1882–1895*. Philadelphia: J. B. Lippincott Company, 1962.

————. *Henry James: The Treacherous Years, 1895–1901*, Philadelphia: J. B. Lippincott Company, 1969.

(These four volumes are part of a definitive biography, not yet complete.)

————, ed. *The Diary of Alice James.* New York: Dodd, Mead & Company, 1964.

Edgar, Pelham. *Henry James: Man and Author.* London: Grant Richards, 1927. Boston: Houghton Mifflin Company, 1927.

Grattan, Clinton Hartley. *The Three Jameses: A Family of Minds. Henry James, Sr., William James, Henry James.* New York: Longmans, Green & Co., Ltd., 1932. Reprinted, New York University Press, 1962.

Kelley, Cornelia Pulsifer. *The Early Development of Henry James.* Urbana, Ill.: University of Illinois Press, 1930. Reprinted, 1965.

LeClair, Robert Charles. *The Young Henry James, 1843–1870.* New York: Bookman Associates, 1955.

Matthiessen, F. O. *The James Family.* New York: Alfred A. Knopf, 1947.

Nowell-Smith, Simon. *The Legend of the Master: Henry James.* New York: Charles Scribner's Sons, 1948.

PRINCIPAL STUDIES OF JAMES'S WORK

Books

Anderson, Quentin. *The American Henry James.* New Brunswick, N.J.: Rutgers University Press, 1957.

Andreas, Osborne. *Henry James and the Expanding Horizon.* Seattle: University of Washington Press, 1948.

Beach, Joseph Warren. *The Method of Henry James.* New Haven: Yale University Press, 1918.

Bewley, Marius. *The Complex Fate.* New York: Grove Press, Inc., 1953.

Blackall, Jean Frantz. *Jamesian Ambiguity and "The Sacred Fount."* Ithaca, N.Y.: Cornell University Press, 1965.

Bowden, Edwin T. *The Themes of Henry James.* New Haven: Yale University Press, 1956.

Canby, Henry Seidel. *Turn West, Turn East: Mark Twain and Henry James.* Boston: Houghton Mifflin Company, 1951.

Cargill, Oscar. *The Novels of Henry James.* New York: The Macmillan Company, 1961.

Cary, Elizabeth Luther. *The Novels of Henry James: A Study.* New York and London: G. P. Putnam's Sons, 1905.

Clair, John A. *The Ironic Dimension in the Fiction of Henry James.* Pittsburgh: Duquesne University Press, 1965.

Cranfill, Thomas M. and Robert L. Clark, Jr. *An Anatomy of "The Turn of the Screw."* Austin: University of Texas Press, 1965.

Crews, Frederick C. *The Tragedy of Manners: Moral Drama in the Later Novels of Henry James.* New Haven: Yale University Press, 1957.

Edel, Leon. *Henry James.* University of Minnesota Pamphlets on American Writers. Minneapolis: Univeristy of Minnesota Press, 1960.

————. *The Prefaces of Henry James.* Paris: Jouve et Cie., 1931.

Gale, Robert L. *The Caught Image: Figurative Language in the Fiction of Henry James.* Chapel Hill: University of North Carolina Press, 1964.

————. *Plots and Characters in the Fiction of Henry James.* Hamden, Conn.: Archon Books, 1965.

Garnier, Marie-Reine. *Henry James et la France.* Paris: Champion, 1927.

Geismar, Maxwell. *Henry James and the Jacobites.* Boston: Houghton Mifflin Company, 1963.

Hoffman, Charles G. *The Short Novels of Henry James.* New York: Bookman Associates, 1957.

Holder, Alan. *Three Voyagers in Search of Europe: Henry James, Ezra Pound, and T. S. Eliot.* Philadelphia: University of Pennsylvania Press, 1966.

Holder-Barrell, Alexander. *The Development of Imagery and its Functional Significance in Henry James's Novels.* The Cooper Monographs, No. 3. Bern: Francke Verlag, 1959.

Holland, Laurence B. *The Expense of Vision: Essays on the Craft of Henry James.* Princeton: Princeton University Press, 1964.

Horne, Helen. *Basic Ideas of James's Aesthetics as Expressed in the Short Stories Concerning Artists and Writers.* Marburg: Erich Mauersburger, 1960.

Howells, William Dean. *Discovery of a Genius: William Dean Howells and Henry James,* ed. Albert Mordell. New York: Twayne Publishers, Inc., 1961.

Hueffer (Ford), Ford Maddox. *Henry James: A Critical Study.* New York: Dodd Mead Company, 1916.

Hughes, Herbert L. *Theory and Practice in Henry James.* Ann Arbor: University of Michigan Press, 1926.

Jefferson, D. W. *Henry James.* Writers and Critics Series. Edinburgh: Oliver & Boyd, Ltd., 1960.

————. *Henry James and the Modern Reader.* Edinburgh: Oliver & Boyd, Ltd., 1964.

Krook, Dorothea. *The Ordeal of Consciousness in Henry James.* New York: Cambridge University Press, 1962.

Lebowitz, Naomi. *The Imagination of Loving: Henry James's Legacy to the Novel.* Detroit: Wayne State University Press, 1965.

Levy, Leo B. *Versions of Melodrama: A Study of the Fiction and Drama of Henry James, 1865–1897.* Berkeley: University of California Press, 1957.

Liljegran, Sten Bodvar. *American and European in the Works of Henry James.* Lund: Lund Universitets Arsskrift, 1920.

Lowery, Bruce. *Marcel Proust et Henry James: Une Confrontation.* Paris: Plon, 1964.

Lubbock, Percy. *The Craft of Fiction.* London: Macmillan & Co., 1921, and New York: Charles Scribner's Sons, 1921.

McCarthy, Harold T. *Henry James: The Creative Process.* New York: Thomas Yoseloff, 1958.

McElderry, Bruce R., Jr. *Henry James.* Twayne's Series, No. 79. New York: Twayne Publishers, Inc., 1965.

Marks, Robert. *James's Late Novels: An Interpretation.* New York: William-Frederick Press, 1960.

Matthiessen, F. O. *Henry James: The Major Phase.* New York: Oxford University Press, 1944.

Milano, Paolo. *Henry James: o Il Proscritto Volontario.* Milan: Arnoldo Mondadori, 1948.

Perry, Bliss. *Commemorative Tribute to Henry James.* Academy Notes and Monographs. New York, 1922.

Poirier, Richard. *The Comic Sense of Henry James: A Study of the Early Novels.* New York: Oxford University Press, 1960.

Putt, S. Gorley. *A Reader's Guide to Henry James.* Ithaca, N.Y.: Cornell University Press, 1966, and London: Thames and Hudson, 1966.

Roberts, Morris. *Henry James's Criticism.* Cambridge, Mass.: Harvard University Press, 1929.

Sayre, Robert F. *The Examined Self: Benjamin Franklin, Henry Adams, Henry James.* Princeton: Princeton University Press, 1964.

Sharp, Sister M. Corona. *The "Confidante" in Henry James: Evolution and Moral Value of a Fictive Character.* Notre Dame, Ind.: University of Notre Dame Press, 1965.

Snell, Edwin Marion. *The Modern Fables of Henry James.* Cambridge, Mass.: Harvard University Press, 1935.

Stafford, William T., ed. *James's "Daisy Miller": The Story, The Play, The Critics.* New York: Charles Scribner's Sons, 1963.

Stevenson, Elizabeth. *The Crooked Corridor: A Study of Henry James.* New York: The Macmillan Company, 1949.

Stone, Edward. *The Battle of the Books: Some Aspects of Henry James.* Athens, Ohio: Ohio University Press, 1964.

Swan, Michael. *Henry James.* London: Arthur Baker, 1952.

Vaid, Krishna Baldev. *Technique in the Tales of Henry James.* Cambridge, Mass.: Harvard University Press, 1964.

Waldock, Arthur, J. A. *James, Joyce and Others.* London: Williams & Norgate, Ltd., 1937.

Ward, Joseph A. *The Imagination of Disaster: Evil in the Fiction of Henry James.* Lincoln, Neb.: University of Nebraska Press, 1961.

————. *The Search for Form: Studies in the Structure of James's Fiction.* Chapel Hill: University of North Carolina Press, 1967.

Wegelin, Christof. *The Image of Europe in Henry James.* Dallas: Southern Methodist University Press, 1958.

West, Muriel. *A Stormy Night with "The Turn of the Screw."* Phoenix: Frye and Smith, 1964.

West, Rebecca. *Henry James.* London: Nisbet, 1916.

Wiesenfarth, Joseph. *Henry James and the Dramatic Analogy.* New York: Fordham University Press, 1963.

Wright, Walter J. *The Madness of Art: A Study of Henry James.* Lincoln, Neb.: University of Nebraska Press, 1962.

Collections of Critical Essays

Dupee, F. W., ed. *The Question of Henry James.* New York: Holt, Rinehart and Winston, Inc., 1945.

Edel, Leon, ed. *Henry James: A Collection of Critical Essays.* Englewood Cliffs, N.J.: Prentice-Hall, Inc., 1963.

Hound and Horn. "Homage to Henry James." VII (April–June, 1934), 361–562.

Kenyon Review, The. Henry James No. V (Autumn, 1943), 481–617.

Lebowitz, Naomi, ed. *Discussions of Henry James.* Boston: D. C. Heath and Company, 1962.

Little Review, The. Henry James No. V (August, 1918), 1–64.

Modern Fiction Studies. Henry James Special No. III (Spring, 1957), 1–196.

————. Henry James Special No. XII (Spring, 1966), 1–180.

New Republic, The. Memorial Issue on William and Henry James. CVIII (February 15, 1943).

Essays

Allott, Miriam. "Form versus Substance in Henry James." *Review of English Literature,* III (January, 1962), 53–66.

————. "Symbol and Image in the Later Work of Henry James." *Essays in Criticism,* III (July, 1953), 321–336.

Auden, W. H. "Henry James and the Artist in America." *Harpers,* CXCVII (July, 1948), 36–40.

Bass, Eben. "Dramatic Scene and *The Awkward Age.*" *PMLA,* LXXIX (March, 1964), 148–157.

Beach, Joseph Warren. *The Twentieth Century Novel: Studies in Technique* (New York: Appleton-Century, 1932), pp. 177–228.

Beebe, Maurice. "The Turned Back of Henry James." *South Atlantic Quarterly,* LIII (July, 1953), 321–336.

Bennett, Joan. "The Art of Henry James: *The Ambassadors.*" *Chicago Review,* IX (Winter, 1956), 12–26.

Bethurum, Dorothy. "Morality and Henry James." *Sewanee Review,* XXXI (July, 1923), 324–330.

Bewley, Marius. *The Eccentric Design: Form in the Classic American Novel* (New York: Columbia University Press, 1959), pp. 220–258.

Blackmur, R. P. *The Lion and the Honeycomb: Essays in Solicitude and*

Critique (New York: Harcourt, Brace & World, Inc., 1955), pp. 61–78, 240–288.

Booth, Wayne. *The Rhetoric of Fiction* (Chicago: University of Chicago Press, 1961), pp. 42–50, 339–374, and passim.

Brown, E. K. "James and Conrad." *Yale Review*, XXXV (1946), 265–285.

Buitenhuis, Peter. "Aesthetics of the Skycraper: The Views of Sullivan, James, and Wright." *American Quarterly*, IX (Fall, 1957), 316–324.

————. "From *Daisy Miller* to 'Julia Bride': 'A Whole Passage of Intellectual History,' " *American Quarterly*, XI (Summer, 1959), 136–146.

————. "Henry James on Hawthorne." *New England Quarterly*, XXXII (June, 1959), 207–225.

Cecil, L. Moffit. " 'Virtuous Attachment' in James's *The Ambassadors.*" *American Quarterly*, XIX (1967), 719–724.

Cestre, Charles. "La France dans l'oeuvre de Henry James." *Revue Anglo-Américaine*, X (October, 1932), 1–13, 112–122.

Cook, Albert. "The Portentous Intelligent Stillness: James." *The Meaning of Fiction* (Detroit: Wayne State University Press, 1960), pp. 134–166.

Edel, Leon. "The Architecture of James's 'New York Edition.' " *New England Quarterly*, XXIV (June, 1951), 169–178.

————. "Henry James: The Americano-European Legend." *University of Toronto Quarterly*, XXXVI (1967), 321–324.

————. *The Psychological Novel, 1900–1950* (Philadelphia: J. B. Lippincott Company, 1955), pp. 53–75 and passim.

Edwards, Herbert. "Henry James and Ibsen." *American Literature*, XXIV (May, 1952), 208–223.

Falk, Robert. *The Victorian Mode in American Fiction, 1865–1885* (East Lansing: Michigan State University Press, 1965), pp. 54–91, 138–156.

Fullerton, Morton. "The Art of Henry James." *Quarterly Review*, CCXII (April, 1910), 393–408; and *Living Age*, CCLXV (June 11, 1910), 643–652.

Gibson, Priscilla. "The Uses of James's Imagery: Drama Through Metaphor." *PMLA*, LXIX (December, 1954), 1075–1084.

Gordon, Caroline. "Mr. Verver, Our National Hero." *Sewanee Review*, LXIII (Winter, 1955), 29–47.

Gosse, Edmund. "Henry James." *Aspects and Impressions* (New York: Charles Scribner's Sons, 1922), pp. 17–53.

Greene, Graham. *The Lost Childhood and Other Essays* (London: William Heinemann, Ltd., 1951), pp. 21–50.

Grenander, M. E. "Henry James's Capricciosa: Christina Light in *Roderick Hudson* and *The Princess Casamassima.*" *PMLA*, LXV (June, 1960), 303–319.

Hartsock, Mildred. "The Exposed Mind: A View of *The Awkward Age.*" *Critical Quarterly*, IX (1967), 49–59.

Hoffman, Frederick J. "Freedom and Conscious Form: Henry James and

The American Self." *Virginia Quarterly Review,* XXXVII (Spring, 1961), 269–285.

————. *The Modern Novel in America* (Chicago: Henry Regnery Company, 1951), pp. 1–30.

Josephson, Matthew. *Portrait of the Artist as an American* (New York: Harcourt, Brace & World, Inc., 1930), pp. 70–138, 365–388.

Knights, L. C. "Henry James and the Trapped Spectator." *Explorations: Essays in Criticism* (London: Chatto & Windus, Ltd., 1946), pp. 155–169.

Leavis, F. R. *The Great Tradition: George Eliot, Henry James, Joseph Conrad* (New York: George W. Stewart, Publisher, Inc., 1949), pp. 126–172.

Lerner, Daniel. "The Influence of Turgenev on Henry James." *Slavonic Review,* XX (December, 1941), 28–54.

Lewis, R. W. B. *Trials of the Word: Essays in American Literature and the Humanistic Tradition* (New Haven: Yale University Press, 1965), pp. 77–96, 116–128.

Matthiessen, F. O. *American Renaissance* (New York: Oxford University Press, 1941), pp. 292–305 and passim.

Melchiori, Giorgio. "Cups of Gold for the Sacred Fount: Aspects of James's Symbolism." *Critical Quarterly,* VII (Winter, 1965), 301–316.

Morris, Wright. *The Territory Ahead* (New York: Harcourt, Brace & World, Inc., 1958), pp. 93–112, 187–214.

Murray, Donald M. "Henry James and the English Reviewers, 1882–1890." *American Literature,* XXIV (March, 1952), 1–20.

O'Connor, Frank. "Transitions: Henry James." *The Mirror in the Roadway: A Study of the Modern Novel* (New York: Alfred A. Knopf, 1956), pp. 223–236.

Poulet, Georges. *Studies in Human Time* (Baltimore: Johns Hopkins University Press, 1956), pp. 350–354.

Pound, Ezra. "Henry James." *Make It New* (New Haven: Yale University Press, 1935), pp. 251–307.

Powers, Lyall H. "Henry James's Antinomies." *University of Toronto Quarterly,* XXXI (January, 1962), 125–135.

————. "Henry James and Zola's *Roman expérimental.*" *University of Toronto Quarterly,* XXX (October, 1960), 16–30.

Rahv, Philip. *Image and Idea: Fourteen Essays on Literary Themes* (New York.: New Directions, 1949), pp. 42–70.

Rouse, H. Blair. "Charles Dickens and Henry James: Two Approaches to the Art of Fiction." *Nineteenth-Century Fiction,* V (September, 1950), 151–157.

Saloman, Roger B. "Realism as Disinheritance: Twain, Howells and James." *American Quarterly,* XVI (Winter, 1964), 531–544.

Schneider, Daniel J. "The Ironic Imagery and Symbolism of James's *The Ambassadors.*" *Criticism,* IX (1967), 174–196.

Short, R. W. "Henry James's World of Images," *PMLA*, LXVIII (December, 1953), 943–960.

————. "Some Critical Terms of Henry James." *PMLA*, LXV (September, 1950), 667–680.

Snow, Lotus. "The Disconcerting Poetry of Mary Temple: A Comparison of the Imagery of *The Portrait of a Lady* and *The Wings of the Dove.*" *New England Quarterly*, XXXI (September, 1958), 312–339.

————. "The Pattern of Innocence through Experience in the Characters of Henry James." *University of Toronto Quarterly*, XXII (April, 1953), 230–236.

————. " 'The Prose and the Modesty of the Matter': James's Imagery for the Artist in *Roderick Hudson* and *The Tragic Muse.*" *Modern Fiction Studies*, XII (Spring, 1966), 61–62.

————. "Some Stray Fragrance of an Ideal: Henry James's Imagery for Youth's Discovery of Evil." *Harvard Library Bulletin*, XIV (Winter, 1960), 107–125.

————. " 'A Story of Cabinets and Chairs and Tables': Images of Morality in *The Spoils of Poynton* and *The Golden Bowl.*" *Journal of English Literary History*, XXX (December, 1963), 413–435.

Spender, Stephen. *The Destructive Element* (London: Jonathan Cape, Ltd., 1935), pp. 23–110, 189–200.

Tanner, Tony. "Henry James." *The Reign of Wonder: Naivity and Reality in American Literature* (New York: Cambridge University Press, 1965), pp. 259–335.

————. "The Watcher from the Balcony: Henry James's *The Ambassadors.*" *Critical Quarterly*, VIII (Spring, 1966), 35–52.

Thurber, James. "The Wings of Henry James." *New Yorker*, XXXV (November 7, 1959), 188–201.

Ticknor, Caroline. "Henry James's *Bostonians.*" *Glimpses of Authors* (Boston: Houghton Mifflin Company, 1922), pp. 243–256.

Van Ghent, Dorothy. *The English Novel: Form and Function* (New York: Holt, Rinehart and Winston, Inc., 1953), pp. 221–228, 428–439.

Warren, Austin. *The New England Conscience* (Ann Arbor: University of Michigan Press, 1967), pp. 143–156.

Watt, Ian. "The First Paragraph in *The Ambassadors:* An Explication." *Essays in Criticism*, X (July, 1960), 250–274.

Wegelin, Christof. "The Rise of the International Novel." *PMLA*, LXXVII (June, 1962), 305–310.

Wellek, Rene. "Henry James." *A History of Modern Criticism, 1750–1950* (New Haven: Yale University Press, 1965), IV, 213–237.

Willett, Maurita. "Henry James's Indebtedness to Balzac." *Revue de Littérature Comparée*, XLI (1967), 204–227.

Winters, Yvor. *In Defense of Reason* (Denver: University of Denver Press, 1947), pp. 300–343.

Woolf, Virginia. "Henry James." *The Death of the Moth and Other Essays* (London: Hogarth Press, Ltd., 1942), pp. 129–155.

Zabel, Morton D. "Henry James: The Act of Life." *Craft and Character in Modern Fiction* (New York: The Viking Press, Inc., 1957), pp. 114–143.

——. "Introduction." *The Portable Henry James* (New York: The Viking Press, Inc., 1951; rev. 1956), pp. 1–29.

INDEX

Aeneid, The, 103
Alexander, George, 25–26
allegory, 2, 47, 48–49, 85
Arnold, Matthew, 13
  Hebraism and Hellenism, 4
art versus the world, 100 and *passim*
authoritarian control, 2; *see also*
  conscience, convention, duty,
  law, manners

Balzac, Honoré de, 11, 12, 18, 33–
  34, 87, 88–89, 127
  Comédie Humaine, La, 130
being versus doing, 4, 5, 23, 99, 103–
  111, 114–116, 118
Besant, Walter, 18
Blake, William, 2, 73, 87, 95,
  Book of Thel, The, 4, 96–97
  Songs of Innocence and Expe-
  rience, 2, 3
Bourget, Paul, 24

child-heroes, 28–29
Civil War, the, 11, 37
Compton, Edward, 20, 24
Conrad, Joseph, 5
conscience (especially New England conscience), 89, 123; *see*
  also convention, duty, law,
  manners
consciousness, 4, 5, 93–94; *see also*
  vision
convention, 5, 66–67, 68; *see also*
  conscience, duty, law, manners

Daudet, Alphonse, 14, 17, 19
dilemma of the artist, 40 ff., 100 ff.,
  121, 123
dramatic, the (as a characteristic
  of fiction), 27, 29–30, 129, 130,
  137–138, 140, 147
duty, 3, 43, 55, 64, 69, 73, 108, 110,
  119; *see also* conscience, convention, law, manners; *cf.* impulse

Eliot, George, 12, 16, 127
  Daniel Deronda, influence on *The*
  Portrait of a Lady, 16
Emerson, Ralph Waldo, 2, 3
emotional cannibalism, 69, 76; *see*
  also manipulation, use
esthetic, James's, 126 ff.
Europeanized American, the, 43,
  48, 52, 53, 54, 60, 62
experimental novel, 117; *see also*
  Naturalism, Zola

Fielding, Henry, 96
Flaubert, Gustave, 14, 134–135
Flaubert group, the, 18; *see also*
  "the grandsons of Balzac," the
  new votaries of realism
Forbes-Robertson, Johnston, 35
form (especially in fiction), 133–
  136
Frohman, Charles, 35

Gardner, Isabella (Mrs. Jack), 24
"grandsons of Balzac, the," 14, 17,
  19; *see also* the Flaubert group,
  the new votaries of realism

161

Hamlet, 126–127

Hawthorne, Nathaniel, 2, 3, 12, 129
  Marble Faun, The, 2, 13, 40, 115

Howells, William Dean, 88

Huckleberry Finn, 5

Ibsen, Henrik, 35

imagination and fancy, 127

impulse, 4, 56, 108, 110, 120; *see also* moral spontaneity, innocence; *cf.* duty

innocence (frequently contrasted with experience), 3, 49, 50, 53, 55, 58, 61, 68, 69, 73, 80, 84, 86, 87, 95–97; *see also* impulse, moral spontaneity

integrity, artistic, 128–129

international fiction, 13, 20, 33, 40 ff.; *see also* international scene, international theme

international scene, 1; *see also* international fiction, international theme

international theme, 114–115, 121, 123; *see also* international fiction, international scene

James, Alice, 19, 24

James, Henry, works of
  Ambassadors, The, 6, 33, 88–94, 97, 130, 135, 139, 140, 143–147
  American, The, 6, 45–49, 78
  American, The (play), 21, 23
  "Americans Abroad," 49–50
  "Art of Fiction, The," 18, 94, 127–128, 132
  Awkward Age, The, 32, 139–140
  Bostonians, The, 17, 19, 20, 117–121
  "Broken Wings," 101–102
  "Bundle of Letters, A," 88–89, 140
  "Coxon Fund, The," 106

Daisy Miller, 5, 52–54, 77

"Death of the Lion, The," 101, 102

"Europe," 76–77

Europeans, The, 54–57, 87, 89

"Fiction and Sir Walter Scott," 127

"Figure in the Carpet, The," 102–103

"Four Meetings," 50–52, 89

"Georgina's Reasons," 80

Golden Bowl, The, 33, 74, 94–98

"Great Good Place, The," 111

"Gustave Flaubert," 135–136

"Guy Domville," 25–27

Hawthorne, 16

"International Episode, An," 57–60

In the Cage, 141–142

"Is There a Life After Death?" 3, 93–94

Lady Barberina, 78–79

"Lesson of Balzac, The," 33

"Lesson of the Master, The," 120

"Liar, The," 113–114, 141

"Madonna of the Future, The," 104–105

"*Nana*," 16

"New Novel, The," 128

New York Edition, the, 33, 34, 134, 148

"Next Time, The," 27, 105–106

Notes of a Son and Brother, 10, 36

Outcry, The, 35–36

"Pandora," 77–78

"Passionate Pilgrim, A," 44–45

Portrait of a Lady, The, 6, 15, 16, 60–75, 76, 81, 84, 85, 86, 87, 95, 97, 114

Princess Casamassima, The, 19, 121–125

"Private Life, The," 111

"Pupil, The," 75–76

"Real Right Thing, The," 102

James, Henry (*cont.*)
  "Real Thing, The," 112–113, 131
  Roderick Hudson, 13, 40–44
  Sacred Fount, The, 32, 143
  Small Boy and Others, A, 36
  "Solution, The," 141
  Spoils of Poynton, The, 6, 123–125
  Tragic Muse, The, 19, 23, 102, 103, 107–111, 118, 120
  "Tree of Knowledge, The," 106
  Turn of the Screw, The, 3, 142–143
  Watch and Ward, 13
  What Maisie Knew, 32, 139–140
  Whole Family, The, (James's chapter, "The Married Son"), 34
  Wings of the Dove, The, 6, 33, 76, 79–87, 94–95
James, Henry, Senior (father), 2, 4, 9, 10, 16, 115–116
James, Mrs. Henry, Senior (mother), 16
James, William, 36

Kemble, Fanny, 13

La Farge, John, 11
Lamb House, Rye, Sussex, 30–32, 34, 36, 37–38
law, 4, 99; *see also* conscience, convention, duty, manners
lionization, 101–103, 110
London, 14, 17, 36
love, 5, 65, 72–75, 76, 85, 97, 98–99

manipulation (of others' lives), 3, 60, 64, 81, 95; *see also* emotional cannibalism, use
manners, 44–45, 49, 54, 56, 57, 60, 61, 86; *see also* conscience, convention, duty, law
Maupassant, Guy de, 14

metaphoric fiction, 2, 44–45, 48, 60, 68, 72–75, 86, 98, 110
Milton, John, 2, 3, 4
  Areopagitica, 2
morality, 4, 5, 87, 93–94, 97–98, 115, 126, 132
moral spontaneity, 61, 90, 95, 98; *see also* impulse, innocence

names (James's artistic use of), 47, 133
narrative authority, 141, 142–144
narrative focus, 32; *see also* point of view
narrative technique, 137 ff.
Naturalism, 17, 19, 78, 117; *see also* experimental novel, Zola
Newport, Rhode Island, 10, 11, 57, 58–59
new votaries of realism, the, 15; *see also* the Flaubert group, "the grandsons of Balzac"
Noakes, Burgess, 38
note-taking, 130–131

omniscient author, the, 129, 137
organic unity (in fiction), 18, 132

Paris, 14
point of view, 137–139, 143–147; *see also* narrative focus
psychological fiction, 6, 7
psychological realism, 142, 143, 147

realism, 15, 16, 18, 48, 126, 127–128
reflexive characterization, 141
religious imagery, 66–74, 85, 96, 101, 106–109
Robins, Elizabeth, 24
Rome, 12–13
Rye, Sussex, 30–32

Scott, Sir Walter, 127
self-knowledge, 3, 4

self-reliance (or self-trust), 3, 4,
    65, 122
sex, 6, 74, 82, 84, 90, 92, 95–96,
    97, 118
Stevenson, Robert Louis, 19
Story, William Wetmore, 13

Temple, Mary (Minny), 11, 12–13,
    32–33, 61, 79–80, 85–86
things, 6, 83, 124–125
Turgenev, Ivan, 14
    On the Eve, influence on *The
    Portrait of a Lady*, 16
    Sportsman's Sketches, 128
Twain, Mark, 126, 132

use, 68, 84, 112; *see also* emotional
    cannibalism, manipulation

Valentine and Orson, influence on
    The American, 46
Venus, 103
vision, 53, 57, 84, 89, 90–93, 96,
    97–98, 144–147; *see also* con-
    sciousness

Woolson, Constance Fenimore, 21,
    25
World War I, 37–38
worldliness, 2, 68, 70–71, 75, 76,
    81–82, 84, 85, 86, 98

Zola, Émile, 14, 15, 19, 117; *see
    also* experimental novel, Na-
    turalism
    Nana, 16
    Rougons-Macquart, Les, 130